Strategies for Child Welfare Professionals Working with Transgender and Gender-Expansive Youth

Strategies for Child Welfare Professionals Working with Transgender and Gender-Expansive Youth

A PRACTICAL GUIDE FOR PROFESSIONALS WORKING
WITH TRANSGENDER AND GENDER-EXPANSIVE YOUTH

GERALD P. MALLON, DSW

Jessica Kingsley Publishers
London and Philadelphia

First published in Great Britain in 2021 by Jessica Kingsley Publishers
An Hachette Company

1

Copyright © Gerald P. Mallon 2021

A CIP catalogue record for this title is available from the
British Library and the Library of Congress

ISBN 978 1 78775 388 4
ISBN 978 1 78775 389 1

Printed and bound in the United States by Integrated Books International

Jessica Kingsley Publishers' policy is to use papers that are natural,
renewable and recyclable products and made from wood grown in
sustainable forests. The logging and manufacturing processes are expected
to conform to the environmental regulations of the country of origin.

Jessica Kingsley Publishers
Carmelite House
50 Victoria Embankment
London EC4Y 0DZ

www.jkp.com

For Wendell Glenn and Inkera Hilliard

Contents

Acknowledgements

In 1987, I started working as the director of a group residence for teenagers in foster care, called the Gramercy Residence, at an agency named Green Chimneys Children's Services in New York City, where I directed a program for gay youth in foster care. Thinking back to that time, more than three decades ago, we rarely spoke about bisexual youth, we didn't at the time work with young lesbians, and there was little, if any, information to inform our practice with transgender or gender-expansive (T/GE) youth. Even though I thought I was fairly knowledgeable about gay and lesbian youth, I was woefully ignorant about the experiences of transgender and gender-expansive youth. But one sunny afternoon in 1993, while having lunch at a taco stand on Santa Monica Boulevard in Los Angeles, with my colleague Wendell Glenn, my entire world view about what it meant to be a trans person changed in an instant. It was one of those experiences that one remembers forever, because it was so illuminating that it caused me to radically change what I thought I knew—into what was valid, accurate and true.

Prior to 1993, I had of course worked with youth who self-identified as transgender but I have to admit that I really did not understand their experience, as much as they tried, many times, to explain it to me. I kept thinking (erroneously now, I know) that these young people who were telling me they were trans were just another version of gay young people. In fact, prior to my illuminating experience with Wendell, Inkera, one of my young people at Green Chimneys, had tried very diligently to get me to understand her experience, but I just did not get it until that day at the taco stand with Wendell. When Wendell, so openly and honestly, talked to me about being a "plain clothes" transgender person, and gave me permission to ask all the questions I had been wanting to ask but felt were too impolite to voice, my mind was opened forever and my journey towards more fully understanding the experiences of T/GE people began. Because Wendell was a colleague and not a client, I could hear what he was telling me, but sadly—and I still regret it to this day—I could not hear what my clients had been trying to tell me. I was not open to hearing them because, I am embarrassed to say, I was pathologizing their identity and not fully accepting them as they told me they were.

But in listening to Wendell, I realized, who was I to pathologize a colleague? Wendell was as sane as I was and so I listened and learned from him in a very different way. For the first time, I had to suspend what I thought I knew about gender identity and sexuality and see things through a different lens. I am ashamed to say that I had not been listening to Inkera, but as soon as I returned home to New York, I asked her if we could meet and I apologized for not being able to hear what she had been telling me for so long. In true Inkera fashion, she immediately gave me forgiveness and said, "Well, it's about time you got it—thank God for Wendell Glenn."

Therefore, it is only right and fitting that I dedicate this book, with love and enormous gratitude, to the two people who have helped me in my journey more than any others—Wendell Glenn and Inkera Hilliard.

I am grateful, too, to my many wonderful colleagues at what I think of as the finest school of social work in the country—The Silberman School of Social Work at Hunter College—for allowing me to be part of a nurturing environment and for giving me a wonderful place to call home for almost 30 years.

Finally, my thanks and deep gratitude to my husband, Martin, who is so patient with all of my travel and my need to isolate when I am writing, and who makes every day a joy because he is a wonderful, loving man. To my chosen family—Nancy, Laura, Lynne, Leslie and Sam—who love me and give me a life and meaning outside my work, my gratitude for their love is inestimable.

Introduction: Preparing to Work with T/GE Youth

We used to have a lot of gay and lesbian youth in our program and I think we did a pretty good job working with them, but then we started to have more transgender youth admitted to our facility and we were not as knowledgeable about how to work with them.

Training participant in a Child Welfare Agency

This book is designed as a practical guide for child welfare professionals interested in increasing their knowledge and skills in working with transgender and gender-expansive (T/GE) youth and their families. T/GE children and youth, and families affected by issues of gender identity expression, are present in every youth service system worldwide, and although much has changed in the past decades (Mallon, 2009) many professionals continue to have inadequate knowledge about how to work effectively with T/GE youth (Shelton, 2015, 2016). As such, T/GE youth continue to be an invisible and underserved population. Consequently, most child welfare professionals and youth workers are not usually well prepared to address or respond to their needs.

Although T/GE youth remain invisible populations for many, the reality is, if you work with adolescents, then you are most likely already working with T/GE youth. This book, which consists of ten chapters and two appendices, is designed to provide professionals with accurate basic information about T/GE youth, including actual case examples. Most chapters also include a section called "What can youth workers do?" that spotlights strategies and concrete actions youth workers can take to help T/GE youth.

The first chapter provides readers with information about the basics of working with T/GE young people. Chapter 2 focuses on the critical issues surrounding the developmental process of forming a T/GE identity, and touches on family issues and some mental health issues. Chapter 3 explores transition issues, social and medical, as they relate to T/GE youth. The myriad of issues related to education for T/GE youth are discussed in Chapter 4. Chapter 5 examines the destructive role that discrimination and anti-T/GE harassment and violence plays in the lives of T/GE youth. The need to create healthy social environments for T/GE youth is explored in Chapter 6. In Chapter 7, I review the central developmental appropriateness of relationships and dating. Chapters 8 and 9 specifically examine the array of unique issues for T/GE youth and youth workers who work with them in child welfare and runaway and homeless youth systems. The final chapter examines the steps organizations must take to become trans-affirming. A detailed glossary of terms and expressions is found in Appendix A. A resources list of websites, programs and films is found in Appendix B; bear in mind, however, that the availability of resources like these changes rapidly. Scholarly research, books and other publications directly referred to within the text are cited in the References section.

This guide is written from a trans-affirming perspective of gender identity expression, which views T/GE identity from an amoral position—as a natural and normal variation of gender orientation, which is not pathologized. The data presented here is practice-based evidence, representative of the current thinking of leading experts practicing with, and in many cases researching, T/GE youth and their families. The case examples utilized to illustrate points throughout represent actual T/GE youth with whom I have had the opportunity to work. These cases, which exemplify the actual experiences of youth in a wide variety of youth service settings, were gathered as part of my work as consultant, trainer, researcher and practitioner around the United States and internationally. The names of these young people—Ariel, Carter, Dane, Denver, Emerson, Finley, Lauren, Lee, Petra, Phoenix, Quinn, Sawyer, Tanner and Tracy—and their families have been altered to protect their confidentiality, and agency names and locations have been removed.

CHAPTER 1

The Basics

I tried to tell them that I was trans, but they had no idea what it meant to be trans. They just kept saying—You're gay, what is this T/GE stuff?

The quote above, taken from prior research on T/GE youth in juvenile justice systems (Mallon & Perez, 2020), aptly expresses one young person's frustration in getting adults to believe that they are T/GE. Youth workers can probably relate to this situation, as surely many have asked themselves at one time or another: Is this youth really T/GE? Is it possible for a young person to identify as T/GE?

This chapter includes basic material needed by social service and child welfare professionals to work compassionately and effectively with T/GE youth.

To clarify discussions in this publication, I have provided, from the start, some definitions that will be helpful to child welfare professionals who may not have a background in or much knowledge of these issues and the lived experiences of T/GE young people. A fuller glossary of terms is provided in Appendix A. However, do remember that brief descriptions of human behavior and gender/sexual identities may not capture all the nuances that are evolving in this field.

Relevant terms and definitions related to T/GE youth

This section outlines key definitions and clarifications of some terminology crucial to framing the T/GE experience. This is not exhaustive, and language is constantly changing. Language, in its most pure and unadulterated form, aids in our connection to each other and the entire universe. A sense of self—an awareness and security in that cultivated identity—is an essential developmental stage. Having that identity mirrored back and affirmed by sociocultural value systems reduces mental, physical and emotional dysregulation (Katz-Wise *et al.*, 2017). A signifier of identity validation is being able to apply, produce and echo language a client uses to describe themselves and their lived experiences. Correct personal gender pronoun/name usage and a baseline understanding of T/GE terminology is a starting point for engagement and professional competency (Russell *et al.*, 2018).

Affirmed gender: The process of bringing the gender role and appearance into alignment with the gender identity, which "affirms" that identity. Thus, the term "affirmed" gender is now becoming more common in describing an individual's gender status.

Cisgender: Describes a person who identifies and expresses a gender that is consistent with the culturally defined norms of the sex they were designated at birth.

Gender diverse: Describes people with gender behaviors, appearances or identities that are incongruent with those culturally designated to their birth sex. Gender-diverse individuals may refer to themselves with many different terms, such as T/GE, non-binary, genderqueer, gender fluid, gender creative, gender independent and non-cisgender. "Gender diverse" is used to acknowledge and include the vast diversity of gender identities that exists. It replaces the former term "gender nonconforming," which has a negative and exclusionary connotation.

Gender dysphoria: A clinical symptom that is characterized by a sense of alienation to some or all of the physical characteristics or social roles of one's designated gender. Also, gender dysphoria is the psychiatric diagnosis in the *Diagnostic and Statistical Manual of Mental Disorders, Fifth Edition (DSM-5)* (American Psychiatric Association, 2013), which has a focus on the distress that stems from the incongruence between one's expressed or experienced (affirmed) gender and the gender assigned at birth. This diagnosis replaced gender identity disorder in the *DSM-5*.

Gender expansive: Conveys a wider, more flexible range of gender identity and/or expression than typically associated with the binary gender system.

Gender expression: Refers to the ways in which people externally communicate their gender identity to others through behavior, clothing, hairstyles, voice and other forms of presentation. Gender expression also works the other way as people assign gender to others based on their appearance, mannerisms, and other gendered characteristics. Gender expression should not be viewed as an indication of sexual orientation.

Gender identity: The individual internal concept of self in terms of female, male, non-binary or gender expansive (a blend, neither, both or more than we have language for). Gender identity is in an internal working model for how the gender(s) of a person relates to the world at large, and it does not need to be reflected or justified by social, medical and political structures (Butler, 1999). Gender identity may match or be different from sex designated at birth (Brown, Herman & Park, 2017; Levitt, 2019).

Non-binary: Most people—including most T/GE people—identify as either male or female, but some people don't neatly fit into the categories of "male" or "female." Some people have a gender that blends elements of maleness or femaleness, or a gender that is different from either male or female. Some people don't identify with any gender. Some people's gender changes over time. People whose gender is not male or female use many different terms to describe themselves, with non-binary being one of the most common. Some non-binary people may feel comfortable within T/GE communities and find this is a safe space to be with others who don't identify as cis, but this isn't always the case. Most T/GE people do not identify as non-binary. While some T/GE people are non-binary, most T/GE people have a gender identity that is either male or female, and should be treated like any other man or woman.

Sex designated at birth (SDB): The social, medical and political enforcement of binary sex classification based on visible or assumed primary or secondary sexual characteristics, for example female or male, when someone is born (Brown *et al.*, 2017). SDB appears on official documents, job applications, medical files and school records. How to make changes to these documents varies by state, and requirements involve multiple obstacles and hoops in order for gender identity to be affirmed and validated by sociopolitical institutions (Movement Advancement Project [MAP], 2020).

Sexual orientation: Separate from gender identity, this refers to how one identifies regarding the people to whom one is sexually, romantically or affectionally attracted. Orientation is not dependent on physical experience, but rather on feelings and attractions. This typically includes lesbian, gay, bisexual, pansexual, omnisexual, asexual, aromantic and queer.

T/GE: "T/GE" or "trans" are often used as umbrella terms to include many different gender identities: T/GE, non-binary, gender diverse. I recognize that not all non-binary and gender-diverse people identify as trans, and it is not my intention to leave anyone out of this discussion. For the purposes of this publication, I will use the abbreviation T/GE to include the experiences of non-binary and gender-diverse people and to move away from a white, Western understanding of binary gender.

The scholarship about T/GE people is growing (Becerra-Culqui *et al.*, 2018; Brill & Kenney, 2016; Brill & Pepper, 2008; Davis, 2008; De Vries, Cohen-Kettenis & Delemarre-Van de Waal, 2006; Edwards-Leeper, Leibowitz & Sangganjanavanich, 2016; Ehrensaft, 2011, 2012, 2014, 2016; Israel & Tarver, 1998; Krieger, 2017; Lev, 2004; Mallon, 2009; Nealy, 2019; Shelton, 2015, 2016; Tannehill, 2019). With this, and society gradually becoming more affirming about the experiences of T/GE young people, child welfare and other social services professionals are afforded greater opportunities to gain knowledge about practicing more competently with T/GE young people.

Interacting with T/GE young people

Some child welfare professionals may have some knowledge of working with lesbian, gay and bisexual youth, but less information about the realities of T/GE youth, whom they may come in contact with in group homes, congregate care settings and foster families. This section includes basic introductory information on respectfully interacting with T/GE young people on a one-to-one basis or in a small group.

No two T/GE young people are exactly the same, and different T/GE young people may use different words to describe themselves. You should follow the lead of each young person, as they will know the language and terms that fit best and feel right to them.

Many professionals struggle over which personal gender pronouns to use with young T/GE people. A basic premise is: if you don't know what personal gender pronouns to use, ask. A simple way to see what personal gender pronouns someone uses—he/him/his, she/her/hers, they/them/theirs or something else—is to wait and see if it comes up naturally in conversation. If you're still unsure, ask politely and respectfully, without making a big deal about it. Sharing your own personal gender pronouns is a great way to bring up the topic—for example, "Hi, I'm Rebecca and I use she/her/hers as my personal gender pronouns. How about you?" If you accidentally use the wrong personal gender pronouns, apologize and move on. Making a big deal out of a personal gender pronoun mistake may be awkward and often draws unwanted attention to the T/GE young person.

There are many topics—social transition, medical transition, sexual activity—that you may be curious about. Be careful and considerate about what other questions you ask. That doesn't mean it's appropriate to ask a T/GE young person about these issues, or expect a T/GE person to be comfortable sharing intimate details about themselves. There are two questions you can ask yourself that may help determine if a topic is appropriate to bring up.

First, "Do I need to know this information to treat them respectfully?" Asking someone's name and personal gender pronoun is almost always appropriate, as we use that information in talking to and about each other every day. Beyond that, though, you may be curious about questions that are not things you truly need to know. For example, a T/GE co-worker's surgical history is rarely information that you need to know.

Second, "Would I be comfortable if this question was turned around and asked of me?" Another good way to determine if a question is appropriate is to think about how it would feel if someone asked you something similar. For example, it would probably not feel appropriate for a co-worker to ask you about your private areas of your body. Likewise, it's probably not appropriate to ask similar questions about a T/GE co-worker's body.

A young person's T/GE identity is their private information to share, or not. A T/GE person may choose not to tell others that they are T/GE because it is unsafe to do so, because they're worried they'll be mistreated or fired, or simply because they don't want to share that information with someone. T/GE young people should be the ones to decide how much information is being shared—a T/GE young person may be open about their identity, but only want to discuss medical issues with certain close friends.

It's a good idea to avoid giving compliments or advice based on stereotypes about T/GE people, or about how men and women should look or act. People sometimes intend to be supportive but unintentionally hurt T/GE people by focusing on their looks or whether they conform to gender stereotypes.

In working with T/GE youth, youth workers need to be clear—both for themselves and their young clients—that gender identity expression and sexuality involve many aspects of identity and relationship that go beyond outward appearance.

WHAT CAN YOUTH WORKERS DO?

One of the best ways of preparing to work with T/GE youth is to examine your own issues with respect to T/GE people. All of us who work with clients walk around with what I call "the big red button" on the top of our heads. That is my visual metaphor for the one (or more) personally sensitive point that triggers a personally based, emotional reaction. Knowing the issues that set you off—that push your button—is crucial to good practice. Although it is not always possible to avoid the emotional issues that upset us when dealing with clients, it is feasible and imperative to develop a sense of mastery over our reactions to the feelings that these sensitive issues trigger. For professionals, openly acknowledging and addressing these issues with a supervisor or a close colleague is a challenge. But also for professionals, it is critical to be self-reflective and to work on development of a professional sense of self, which includes a heightened sense of self-awareness. Allowing personal issues to cloud one's judgment when working with a client is unethical and wrong.

Conclusion

Like all young people, T/GE youth are entitled to bias-free attention to their unique needs and to be safe when accessing services in youth-orientated organizations. They should be supported in their gender identity and never required to conform to traditional conceptions of gender in order to receive appropriate services. Youth care professionals who work with T/GE young people should be educated about the wide range of T/GE issues, should know the differences between the myths and stereotypes from the reality of a T/GE young person's life and be prepared to work sensitively and competently with these young people. Knowledge about lesbian, gay and bisexual issues may be helpful in working with T/GE young people, but gender identity issues are very different from issues related to sexual orientation.

The next chapter will address the issues relevant to the developmental process of forming a T/GE identity.

CHAPTER 2

The Developmental Process of Forming a T/GE Identity

There are many pathways to a developmental process of a T/GE identity. The classic narrative is that the individual knew that they were "different" even as a child, they struggled with people telling them that they were not who they knew they were, they persevered, finally transitioned to their affirmed gender identity and their lives moved forward. And while this is the narrative for some T/GE people, other T/GE people do not have this experience until later in their lives. Others may live their lives as non-T/GE people before coming to the realization that they are in fact transgender or gender expansive. Still others may transition socially, but not physically. Professionals who work with T/GE youth must keep in mind that each person's story may be different and each is valid.

This chapter will explore the developmental process of forming a T/GE identity for young people. We will begin by examining the various developmental pathways, and move from there to examining the coming-out process for T/GE young people. We will conclude by highlighting what youth workers can do to facilitate the coming-out experience for the T/GE youth with whom they work.

Various developmental pathways

Krieger (2017) offers a range of developmental pathways to be considered by clinicians, namely early awareness, awareness at puberty and later awareness. These are highlighted below with some modifications.

Early awareness

Children know from very early ages—in fact, gender designation starts for many in utero—what boys are expected to do and what girls are expected to do. Boys are blue, girls are pink. Various cultures may have different gender expectations, but they also have expectations for what behaviors are gender affirming and clear guidance about how far from the "norm" someone might stray with respect to their designated gender.

Some research (Drescher & Pula, 2014; Wallien & Cohen-Kettenis, 2008) has suggested that if gender-variant children are followed from childhood into adulthood, only some will identify as T/GE. Ehrensaft (2012, 2016) and Steensma and colleagues (2013), however, found different results which suggest that there was a higher intensity of body discomfort and greater focus on gender issues. In fact, Ehrensaft (2012, p.346) notes that:

> a child who is not allowed to express gender in the ways that feels right to him or her often shows signs of stress, distress or behavioral disruption. Once allowed to transition, these children typically relax and the signs of stress, distress and disruption dissipate if not disappear altogether.

Adolescents experience huge changes in every facet of their lives as they transition from childhood to adulthood. The narrative of Ariel speaks emphatically to this phenomenon:

> When I was very little, probably about four or five, I just kept telling everyone that I was a girl, not a boy. The more that my parents and caregivers told me that I was not, the more upset I became. It wasn't just a matter of not getting my way, I was deeply distressed. My mom, seeing how upset I was almost every day, bless her, convinced my dad when I was about nine years old to let me dress the way I wanted to—at home. They also let me be called by my girl name. That was such a relief for me; even though at school and outside I still had to dress like a boy and be called by my boy name, at least I had some place where I could be myself and that helped me so much.

Ariel, fortunately, had family support to live at least part time in her affirmed gender, and clearly had certainty about this before reaching puberty. T/GE young people who make the transition before puberty are able to take advantage of medical interventions that allow them to have a puberty that is more in sync with their cisgender peers. The story of Jazz Jennings (2016) and the TV series documenting her early transition (James, Miller & St. John, 2018) provides another version of this narrative of early awareness.

Awareness at puberty

Puberty may exacerbate a young T/GE person's distress about their body and their inner feelings about their gender. As bodies of adolescents begin to change and secondary sexual characteristics change in clear, physical ways, T/GE youth may have very strong feelings that these changes, which they cannot control, are not right for them. The narrative of Tanner, a T/GE young person, speaks to these changes:

> When my body started to change around age 12, I remember looking in the mirror and saying—this is not right! It was so upsetting that my body was getting more and more like a male body every day, and I knew inside that I was not a male. There was nothing I could do to stop it, and that for me was just so upsetting. I didn't know at that time what it meant to be trans, I just knew that the changes that were happening to me were very upsetting. As I found out late about what it meant to be a trans person, I began to understand more, but those early days were so sad for me.

Those whose awareness begins in puberty may feel as though they have to catch up. Young people may begin to move towards a social transition (which is discussed in the following chapter), while medical interventions require more preparation and parental consent. Delays in social or medical transitions can be very distressing for T/GE young people. The lack of family support can add to this distress. Peers and other adults, including youth workers and clinical professionals, can provide important support during this period and will have a great impact on whether or not this T/GE teen will be able to thrive as a healthy young person (Aramburu Alegría, 2018).

Later awareness

Those young people who come to an awareness of their emerging gender identity after the onset of puberty will almost certainly be distressed at the physical changes that have already occurred. Once full awareness has occurred, there is an urgency to live within their affirmed gender as soon as possible. They may be distressed about lost time and may be impatient to start the medical transition, if that is what they choose, as soon as possible.

Sawyer's narrative highlights their experiences as one who had a later awareness of their T/GE identity:

> It wasn't like I didn't know I was trans, but my family was so hateful to me that I couldn't address my gender issues at all. Finally, when I was 17, I left home, got a job and started to explore what it would take for me to start the transition process. Of course, I met lots of older trans people who educated me about hormones, and wigs, and make-up and tucking and all of that, but I felt like I had so much to learn. As I was initially transitioning I had some run-ins with women when I tried to use the women's restroom. That was distressing, but I was determined to not let their hostility get to me—the more "real" I became, the less that happened. Now, ten years into my transition, I am confident, assured and feeling good. I wish that I could have done this sooner; all the crap I had to go through could have been lessened if I could have transitioned early, but hey, lessons learned, right?

Gender-expansive and non-binary youth pathways

Gender-expansive and non-binary youth may face challenges that can differ from those discussed above.

Non-binary is a term that covers any gender identity that does not fit the two gender categories of male or female. There is no standard way that a non-binary person looks (Frohard-Dourlent *et al.*, 2017). Most non-binary young people are trying to be comfortable within themselves and try to be understood by those who matter most to them. Most want to live in a world where there are multiple ways to express gender, or not to express gender. Here is how Tracy views the experience of identifying as a non-binary person:

I don't identify as gay, lesbian, bi, trans or male or female. I actually just try to identify as a human. I am about people, not parts. Sometimes people, especially adults, do not take me seriously. They remind me over and over that there are just two genders—male or female—and insist that I should pick one. But they are wrong; there are multiple ways of viewing gender and I just will not be squeezed into a binary either/or box. I am comfortable identifying as human; if they are not okay with this, that is not my problem.

Gender expansive, as defined by Brill and Kenney (2016, p.52), is:

an umbrella term...to describe individuals who broaden their culture's gender norms for identity and expression. It acknowledges that there are many ways in which people stand outside the binary. The term helps to describe and affirm personal experiences and expressions of gender that cannot be positively categorized using existing language. It recognizes that it is society's narrow perceptions of gender and the consequent limitations that it imposes that must be questioned, rather than the individuals who don't conform to them.

In a world where almost every form has just two boxes for gender—"male" or "female"—where many restrooms are clearly marked "men" or "women" and there are no other choices, youth who identify as gender expansive or non-binary are forced over and over again to make a choice. For these young people, neither option fully represents their identities, which can feel like the world is saying, "You don't fit in!"

Non-binary and gender-expansive youth may identify with one or both genders or no gender at all. Some non-binary people may desire physical modification or hormone therapy, some may change their name or undergo personal gender pronoun changes, and some may not.

Coming out as T/GE

Every young person, regardless of gender identity or gender expression, struggles with the seminal developmental tasks of adolescence. Changes in their emotional and physical capacities, and their brain chemistry, and the complex social dynamics they encounter add significant layers to this developmental process. The developmental process of adolescence has been written about elsewhere in great detail, most notably by Brill and Kenney (2016) in their book *The Transgender Teen*, which provides an excellent overview of the goals in adolescent development.

With T/GE youth, these developmental changes also involve supporting their process of personal development and sense of self so that they might feel secure and accepting of their gender identity and expression of gender. Coming out, or disclosing one's T/GE identity, is an additional task for T/GE adolescents and can be one of the most challenging parts of their journey towards authenticity. At the same time, it can be one of the most satisfying and rewarding. The first step that a T/GE person must do is to come out to themselves.

Models of T/GE development

There are several T/GE developmental models (Bockting, 2013; Devor, 2004; Levitt & Ippolito, 2014). All three of these models take a stage approach to conceptualizing a T/GE person's identity. Additionally, they all assume that the transition trajectory is from a female to male or male to female perspective, and do not consider the identity of people who may identify as non-binary (Chang, Singh & dickey, 2018). While each of these models lends merit to the overall conceptualization of T/GE identity development, written by a social worker, from a social work perspective, Lev's model (2004) resonates most robustly for social work professionals.

Brill and Kenney (2016) propose six stages of positive gender identity consolidation:

Stage 1: Dissonance. This is marked by tension and confusion. Some young people may experience a crisis at this stage, and some risky behavior may emerge as a means to managing their feelings of shame, anxiety and low self-esteem as they become more aware of their gender confusion. Tanner expresses their dissonance this way:

> I felt different when I was a child. They kept telling me I was a boy and I should do boy things, but I knew I was a girl and no matter how hard they tried to convince me otherwise, I always felt I was not what they said I was.

Stage 2: Comparison. As the word implies, this is a period of looking at oneself and seeing where one matches or does not match with others. T/GE youth who are coming to acknowledge their gender identity for the first time, or realizing that their feelings about their gender are not going to go away, may find that they have to deal with these feelings. They may compare themselves to others as a means of coming to terms with this awareness. Some may first identify as gay, or lesbian, or bisexual or asexual as they try on other identities, only later realizing that they are actually T/GE, as Emerson recalls in this narrative:

> I had friends in school who were out as gay or lesbian, and, at first, I said I was bi—I had sexual experiences with both guys and girls so I figured I was bisexual. I found I was comparing myself to other girls, not guys. I knew that I felt attracted to girls and thought well maybe I was a lesbian. It didn't occur to me for quite some time that I was really trans.

Stage 3: Tolerance. This is the beginning of making one's way toward self-acceptance. This period is marked by the young person's ability to say, "I am probably T/GE or I am not sure, but I definitely have an issue with gender." Young people in this stage may continue to explore other labels which best fit their internal sense of identity. In some cases, this is less like experimentation and more like a process of elimination as they figure out what identity fits best. Sexuality may be another area that they explore and it may be that through sexual exploration some young people find their best sense of self in relation to their gender. During this stage, young people will try to make meaningful connections to others like them, and will certainly look to the internet to identify others who may be like them (Selke *et al.*, 2020). The presence of an accepting adult who can help create space for them to find a good fit can assuage the feelings of isolation and alienation that some youth experience during this stage, as evidenced by Finley's recollection:

> I had a great mentor while I was going through all of this. My aunt, who I lived with, was always so open and helpful. She was never judgey—she just kept saying as I kept exploring, "Honey, you will find out what feels best for you, don't you worry." That really helped

me stay open and moved me forward to become the person that I am today.

Once these young people begin to recognize and affirm who they are, they are ready to enter the stage of self-acceptance.

Stage 4: Acceptance. This is the stage where T/GE young people are more settled in their identity. They develop their own personal style—grooming, clothes and activities—and are more comfortable with their own gender expression. Normalizing their gender identity, increasing contacts with other T/GE young people and finding themselves more comfortable in the world all move them toward greater self-acceptance, as Finley recalls:

> Honey, let me tell you, when I finally accepted myself, I felt so confident and strong. I was clear about my new name, about what pronouns I used and I felt like I could walk into the subway or down the street with my head held high. It didn't happen overnight, mind you, it took a while, but when it all finally clicked for me, I just felt like a whole person for the first time.

While T/GE youth can look more confident in this phase, it is still an exceptionally vulnerable time for them, as their internal sense of "fit" can be very fragile. A negative reaction from a peer or an adult can crush their new confidence. Rejection from family, peers, staff or communities important to the young person can be devastating. Reaching acceptance is achieved when the young person experiences a sense of wholeness that they have not experienced before.

Stage 5: Pride. This is the point at which T/GE youth appreciate their uniqueness and develop a sense of pride about who they are. There is a shift from the internal work to the external process of connecting with community. This is also the time when young people might begin to address the injustices and inequities of society towards T/GE people, as Dane recounts:

> Once I was clear about who I was—a proud trans person—I became very radical. I was angry about the injustice I saw around me and the

struggle that trans people like me had to go through on a daily basis. I didn't take any crap from people, especially those nasty comments that people sometimes made under their breath. I confronted them each and every time. I know now that that was sometimes dangerous for me, but at the time, I had to respond. Most people just shut right up when I gave it back to them and stood up proud. Now that I am older and I have been out for quite a while, I do not confront every injustice—it's very tiring to do that, and now I save my energy for those things that I want to do that sustain me.

With increased openness comes increased experiences with stigma and discrimination, but unlike the earlier phases where such negative experiences could have caused instability, pride becomes a key factor in developing resilience to these social pollutants.

Stage 6: Consolidation. This is the point at which a person's gender identity is integrated into their other aspects of identity—family, race, ethnicity, culture, religion and social class. The ability to be a multi-dimensional person takes time but brings with it confidence and strength, as Dane remembers:

When I first came out as trans it was not easy. But the longer I have been out, the more comfortable I have become with myself and my identity, and the better things have got. At first, I just wanted to be invisible, then I became more outspoken and in fact kinda "in your face" about my gender identity. But now I am more able to be proud of being a Puerto Rican, a brother, a son and a trans man. It's not just about my trans identity, which is of course important, it is also about all of those other places where I belong too.

Why come out?

Coming out is not a one-time event, but a continuous process that never really ends, one which, it is hoped, becomes easier with time and practice.

The most direct answer about why it is important to come out is that to be out means to be authentic, to be genuine, to get rid of that false sense of self that some people develop before they take their first brave step out of the closet that many have built around themselves. Although gay, lesbian and bisexual people also come out, T/GE people are challenged in coming out by a different set of conditions. Once a T/GE person begins to socially or medically transition from the sex that they were designated at birth, they may also begin to look different and, as such, their appearance will signal a change for family, friends and colleagues to see. The choice of whether or not to disclose is not as readily available for many T/GE people, especially at the beginning of their transition.

Coming out to self

The understanding that one is T/GE can take a short period of time or several decades. In most cases, T/GE people have an idea that they are "different" from their designated gender early on, when they might surmise that something feels "not right" with their bodies. Tanner says it best:

> When I was a young boy, I would look at my genitals in the bathtub and I would think, something is not right. I knew I couldn't say anything about it to anyone, and I knew that my brothers, who always seemed to be talking about their penises, didn't feel the same way. It wasn't until I was 17 or 18 that I started to identify as trans, but when I think back, I realize that I knew something was amiss many years before.

Every person has a different sense of self-awareness for a range of reasons—culture, ethnicity, race, religion, societal pressure. Although many young people, like Tanner, realize that they are different from their siblings or peers at an early age and do not know why they feel as they do, they sense from many subtle and maybe not so subtle messages from family and friends that they should not openly discuss or acknowledge these feelings. They may feel stress in keeping this information hidden, but in moving towards acceptance they will begin to, as therapist Arlene Lev (2004) calls it, "reach out" to share information with others who they tacitly understand may have been in a similar situation and who will be able to provide some support.

Coming out to family and close friends

Although most cisgender individuals go through life without thinking very much about gender or what it might feel like to be a person of T/GE experience, T/GE youth do not have that luxury.

From clinical observation, I sense an increasing number of parents and caregivers who are acknowledging their child's gender struggle, although many T/GE youth may try to keep their gender issues secret until they cannot hold them back any longer.

Denver provides this recollection about coming out to family:

> I never actually came out to my parents. I came out to a close family friend of ours first—he was gay, so I knew he would accept me. I sent him an email and told him that I have always felt like a girl inside, and that I want to get surgery and everything so I can be a normal girl. He told me that he completely supported me, and that I shouldn't be scared of coming out to my parents because they had always suspected I might be trans since I was really little.
>
> Later, my mom read the email when I left my computer on, and she told me that she knew all along that I might be trans, because I used to tell her when I was little that I was supposed to be a girl, her daughter. She didn't know very much about trans youth back then, but she promised to accept me and help me as much as she could. That was two years ago. Now I have been on puberty blockers and hormones for more than a year, I am having surgery in less than a year, and I finally am the girl I have always needed to be.

T/GE young people who do come out to their families do so in a variety of different ways. Some disclose in person, or on the phone, some do it via email or text or letter, or through a third party. Those young people who disclose their T/GE identity to their families may experience a range of reactions, from loving acceptance to complete rejection, and there is often lots of complexity between those two poles (Birnkrant & Przeworski, 2017).

Most parents/caregivers will need time to process this information. Some parents/caregivers feel a sense of loss in the process. A father of a T/GE man may feel as if he has lost his daughter, in spite of the fact that he may be gaining a son (Norwood, 2013). Some parents and caregivers feel guilt, others may find it difficult to talk about their child's disclosure. No matter how obvious the signs may have seemed, disclosure often takes parents/caregivers by surprise. Moms and dads of these kids then must deal not only with shock, denial, loss, anger, grief, misplaced guilt and shame, but also with many real concerns about the safety, health, surgery, employment and potential future love relationships of their child (Boivin *et al.*, 2020; Gray *et al.*, 2016; Wahlig, 2014). It is important to note that when a T/GE person comes out, the entire family system—siblings, grandparents, cousins, aunts/uncles—comes out as well.

Friends of the T/GE person to whom they disclose will also have their own reactions to this new information. While some friends may initially have a negative reaction and then become more supportive over a period of adjustment, others may appear at first to be accepting and then after thinking about it can become uncomfortable and withdraw. Friends have many of the same experiences as do family members, and one thing is for certain, there will be a period of adjustment to this new information, as Sawyer notes in this narrative:

> When I came out, telling my family was the hardest, but after that it got easier. After that, I told friends whom I was close to; most of them were cool with it, but some became a bit more distant, and that hurt. I realized that if I had a good relationship with my friends before I told them, when I finally did tell them, after a couple of questions, they were pretty okay with me—calling me by my new name and pretty much treating me the same way that they had before I came out.

Some T/GE people come out gradually, telling the most important people in their lives first, usually friends. Many T/GE people continue the coming-out process by then gradually telling others—family, co-workers and so on. Coming out, however, is a continual process for people; once T/GE people refuse to hide or masquerade as cisgender people, the opportunities for disclosure are many. Regardless of the reactions from family and friends to a disclosure of their T/GE identity, a T/GE person must face their family, friends, co-workers and acquaintances on a daily basis. For some, the face-to-face contact can be a daunting proposition. As such, email, texting and social network sites can be a very convenient way to come out. One posting or well-written email can reach many people at once and lessen the stress of having to disclose repeatedly. Lee provides this recollection of their coming out via text message:

> When I was ready, rather than telling each person individually, I just decided to send a long text to the important people in my life. I took some time to construct a clear text, explaining that I was coming out as a trans man, telling them that this was something I had been struggling with for quite a while, but being clear that I was no longer struggling—I was sure. I asked people to start using he/him/his pronouns with me and to please call me Lee. The last thing I said was that if anyone had questions or if they wanted to talk to me they should private message me. I'll tell you with one or two exceptions, where I just didn't hear anything from them, most of the people I reached out to were wonderful and supportive.

Being found out is different from coming out in that it is an unplanned disclosure, a situation when a person does not have an option about a planned coming-out experience and they unexpectedly get found out. When this happens in a family, in most cases a crisis situation results. Tracy provides an example of this phenomenon:

> I came home from school one day and found my grandmother who raised me crying at the kitchen table. I was so upset when I saw her that I ran to her and said, "Gran, what's the matter? What happened?" She didn't say anything, she just handed me my bra and my panties. I had hidden them, I thought, in my dresser, but I guess she found them when she was straightening up. When she asked me why I had them, my heart just sank. I knew that things would never again be the same. Now she knew something about me that I wasn't ready to tell her. Things changed after that.

If a young person is "found out" by his or her or their family, the family will need support, assistance and compassionate understanding from those trying to help them. Youth workers will need to know of services in the community and in some cases what types of child welfare services are available where family members can find support, or be prepared to provide it themselves.

Coming out, especially for T/GE youth, can be a very liberating experience. It is like being free after a long imprisonment. Some youth, not yet secure with their newly accepted identity, can go to extremes by dressing differently or acting differently—as some people might say, *flaunting* their identity.

"Flaunting it"

Like their cisgender counterparts, T/GE youth have no desire to make a spectacle of themselves, but they do want to be able to be themselves. What is generally attributed to "flaunting" one's T/GE identity is usually an adaptation to living life openly as a T/GE person. True joy and liberation after a long period of confusion or hiding can lead some T/GE youth to act as if they need to "tell the world" about their gender identity. The discomfort that some observers feel is their unfamiliarity with T/GE people being open about their sexual or gender orientation.

In cases where youth workers have to provide the support, they need to be prepared to provide an array of services to both the youth affected and their family. They might be called on to provide written information to both youth and family members about sexual orientation or gender identity expression issues. They might also have to utilize some crisis intervention strategies for families who are more prone to verbal abuse or physical confrontations. Youth workers might need to find a respite situation (temporary safe housing) or, in some cases, find permanent placement for a youth who has been thrown out of their home, preferably in a family-like situation as opposed to a group home, a congregate care setting or a shelter.

Being found out throws the entire family system—not just the T/GE youth—into crisis, and most families will need assistance to emerge intact from this crisis state. As a youth worker, you might also be called on to assist families in dealing with the reality of having a T/GE family member.

T/GE youth of color are dealing with oppression on multiple levels—race, ethnicity, culture, ability, geography, sexual orientation, gender identity expression—and therefore may have multiple stresses associated with coming out as T/GE (Singh, 2013).

Transitioning

Transitioning is a term used to describe the process of T/GE youth shifting from being seen in the world in their designated sex at birth to moving through the world in their affirmed status (Nealy, 2019, p.63). Nealy differentiates between two distinct aspects of transitioning: *social transition* and *medical transition*. Both will be discussed in the following chapter.

What can youth workers do to assist a T/GE youth with the coming-out process?

When a T/GE young person comes out to a youth professional, it is important, notes Nealy (2019, p.58), to ask a few questions that demonstrate one's understanding, acceptance and compassion. Some of these may be:

- First, thank you for trusting me and for sharing this with me. Has this been a secret that you have kept or have you told anyone else?

- Who else have you shared this news with?

- Do you feel safe at home?

- Do you feel safe at school?

- Do you feel safe in your community?

- Are you supported by any important adults in your life?

- Do you need help of any kind?

- Do you need resources?

- Do you need someone to listen?

It is critical to acknowledge the young person's courage in sharing about their gender identity and expression. Validating the young person's identity by asking and then using their identified name and personal gender pronouns is an important signifier that communicates your acceptance and support. But by far the most important thing that any adult can do when a young person comes out is to listen. You may be the first person that they have told, you may be the first person who has been accepting and affirming, you may be the first person who validates them by asking if there is a name that they prefer other than their birth name. Asking open-ended questions and demonstrating active listening, without judgment, is critical.

The fact that a young person has come out to you does not mean that they are ready to come out to everyone. If and when a young person discusses the possibility of coming out to others in their life, which might include parents/caregivers, teachers, friends and other family members, Nealy (2019) offers, and I have elaborated on, the following points to consider:

- Has the young person thought about where and when to come out to their parents/caregivers/family?

- What does the young person imagine that their response might be?

- Has the family ever discussed T/GE people or issues before? If so, what was the conversation like?

- Are there any other T/GE family members?

- Who in their family might be the most accepting?

- Who might be the least likely to be accepting?

- How would a T/GE young person handle rejections from their parents/caregivers or other family members?

- What would a young person say at that moment of initial disclosure and can you role-play a variety of possible reactions with them?

- Can you, with the young person's permission, invite parents/ caregivers or family members to meet with you and the young person so that the young person can come out with you present to support them and to answer the parents/caregivers' questions and concerns?

- What kind of safety plan does the young person envision—meaning quite literally where would they go if their safety was at risk?

- How might they envision handling the situation if the level of verbal, emotional or physical violence is overwhelming?

- Where would the young person go if their parents/caregivers tell them to leave the home?

- Is there a person (extended family, friend, neighbor) that they could go to if they need to leave their home?

- Would the young person promise to call the worker after the disclosure to tell them how the disclosure and the conversation went?

- Are there things that the young person might still need to work out before disclosing to others?

- What friends might they come out to first and why?

- How might the young person handle personal questions from friends, or respond to bullying?

- How might the young person deal with the reality that their friends might tell others, even if they promise not to?

Role-playing these conversations with friends and parents/caregivers/family can be very useful, as it can help the young person to be clear about what they want to say and how they want to say it. Playing out a range of scenarios is very important, as is practicing what kinds of questions a parent or friend might ask and how they might answer the questions.

Assuring confidentiality is essential when one is addressing coming-out issues. There are some situations where disclosure is necessary, for example if there is self-harm or when a person is threatened. When disclosing seems essential, discussing this need with the young person directly is key. In many cases, it is best to work with the young person to get them to directly share this important information about themselves.

Coming out is a process, which does end with one disclosure. There is never, as Nealy (2019, p.61) notes, "a time when a T/GE person will 'finish' coming out." T/GE people face decisions daily about whether or not to come out about their T/GE history. A T/GE teen in an emergency room or beginning a new intimate relationship has to decide about disclosing their gender identity, and as such, coming out is continuous. It is much more than simply "announcing" your trans or gender-expansive identity.

And finally, it is also important to note that some T/GE young people may no longer perceive coming out as relevant. In their opinion, they may have always been out or they might have come to understand their T/GE identity early on in a more developmentally appropriate and natural way.

As the world becomes more aware of gender identity and T/GE people, the need to come out may be less relevant for T/GE young people. With decreased stigma and increased social acceptance, it is possible that T/GE young people will not face the same coming-out process of "unpacking" their internalized shame about being T/GE or gender expansive.

A few tips on what *not* to say or do when someone comes out to you

- Don't say you always knew.

- Don't say you're pleased they told you, honored even.

- Don't say it doesn't matter to you.

- Don't say it's a phase.

- Don't get offended that they didn't tell you before—it's complicated to disclose.

- Don't feel bad that you need some time to process it—it's a two-way thing.

Conclusion

In this chapter, we explored the developmental issues that exist for T/GE young people. Coming out may be one of the most difficult parts of a T/GE person's journey. But at the same time, it means that T/GE young people can finally live in the world as their true, authentic selves. The chapter that follows is devoted to addressing the social and medical transition issues that face most T/GE young people.

CHAPTER 3

Social and Medical Transition Issues

Introduction

The transition process for T/GE young people usually begins with the social transition and ends when a young person's T/GE identity has remained consistent over time and the youth has demonstrated a positive emotional and social adjustment to their affirmed gender. Medical transition interventions typically include hormone therapies and gender-affirming surgeries. This chapter provides a brief overview of the vital aspects of the social and medical transition processes for T/GE youth. It is important for youth workers working with T/GE youth that they understand these processes, but also that they are able to provide young people with basic information to assist them if they are seeking guidance on issues pertaining to transition. Youth workers should familiarize themselves with some of the common gender-affirming social and medical interventions that T/GE young people may seek so that, when and if they are ready to discuss transitioning, they have a framework for understanding what this entails (Janssen & Leibowitz, 2018). It is the responsibility of the youth worker to have a working knowledge of these interventions, so that the young person is not put in the position of having to educate the youth worker. In addition to the emotional and physiological aspects of social and medical transition, it is also important to discuss with the young person the costs and accessibility issues associated with it.

The purpose of this chapter is not to give the reader a detailed account of all the social and medical procedures that may affect T/GE youth, but to provide a general idea of the usual processes involved. It is important for youth workers to familiarize themselves with gender-affirming interventions so that they may understand what T/GE youth are talking about or dealing with and can provide support, or point them to places where they can obtain accurate information which will ultimately lead them to informed consent (Levine, 2019). Youth workers should know about the benefits and risks for the varied aspects of transition that are available to them as they move towards making decisions now or in the future about their well-being and health (Turban *et al.*, 2020).

Social transition

The tasks usually associated with social transitioning are: readiness to begin the transition; legal name change; and being recognized for one's affirmed gender at school. The process of social transition usually begins as the young person starts to live part time or full time in their affirmed gender. It usually involves taking steps to change one's name (in some cases to do that legally, in other cases just making the change) and to shift to personal gender pronouns that more closely match their affirmed gender. Social transitions generally precede medical transitions and, if necessary, are fully reversible. However, the decision to begin socially transitioning is a huge decision for a young person.

Assessing readiness of the young person is one of the tasks for professionals working with T/GE young people. Although there is no universal timeline, professionals should consider the young person's clarity of their confirmed gender and assess the readiness of their family members, schools, youth programs and other communities that are important to the young person.

Nealy (2019 pp.60–1) offers clear guidance for practitioners and parents/caregivers to assess readiness. These include:

- Does the young person (parents/caregivers) understand the differences between biological sex, gender identity, gender expression and sexual orientation?

- Is the young person aware of the wide range of gender identities and expressions that are possible?

- Are they clear and certain about their affirmed gender identity expression?

- Has their understanding been consistent over some period of time?

- Are they prepared to navigate the steps and tasks involved in a social transition?

- Do they have the information they need for the above?

- Are they prepared to come out to siblings, extended family members, peers, school personnel and other important people in their lives?

- Have they thought about what they will say when they disclose? Have they decided to do this in person or using social media, text or email?

- Are they emotionally ready to disclose?

- Have they considered the range of reactions that they may receive, what questions they might be asked, and thought about how they might want to respond?

- Have they made a safety plan for any possible safety concerns?

- Do they have the support that they need to successfully navigate the transition, especially family support—whether it be family of origin or chosen family?

Readiness for social transition means that everyone has the information that they need to move through the transition process. Readiness means that any questions or concerns have been answered. Role-playing possible scenarios, including positive, negative and neutral reactions, can be very helpful for young people and their families.

Choosing a new name

Social transitions often begin with choosing a new name that more closely matches the young person's sense of their affirmed gender. There are many ways that young people make the decision to choose a new name but usually they know what name they want to begin using and, in some cases, they have been using this name since childhood. The importance of changing their name to match their affirmed status is a significant step for a T/GE young person, as Ariel notes:

> Oh my God, when I started to use my new name—and yes, I did model my name after Ariel the mermaid from the Disney movie; I know it sounds a bit silly, but I liked it, and I still do—I was so happy. I had this dead name that I never related to, and when I got to use my name that I chose, the name that I believe best identifies me, I just felt so good inside.

Over time, the young person who has changed their name may pursue a legal name change so that legal documents (school records, birth certificates, passports, driver's license, social security card) might reflect the name that matches the young person's affirmed gender. An order from a judge in the family's residential jurisdiction is required to legally change one's name. If a young person is considered an adult in that jurisdiction, they can petition the court themselves. When the young person is a minor, the parents/caregivers or guardians must petition the court. Fees are usually involved and some courts require an attorney. A court-ordered name change does not generally change the gender markers on identity documents. Changing gender markers can be regulated by the federal, state or local municipalities. Young people and their families must become familiar with the regulations regarding gender-marker changes. The National Center for Transgender Equality provides links to attorneys in many states that can be hired to assist with changing gender markers on legal documents.[1] Some attorneys from lesbian, gay, bisexual, transgender and questioning/queer (LGBTQ) legal organizations may offer these legal services pro bono.

---

1   https://transequality.org/issues/resources/trans-legal-services-network-directory

Changes in gender expression

Social transition will include changes in the ways that T/GE youth express their gender. Clothing choices, hairstyles, use of jewelry and make-up may all be a part of this process. Some young people make choices that they deem make them appear more masculine or feminine, other youth may be less concerned about binary issues and opt for a more androgynous appearance, rejecting the male or female stereotypical binary and possibly identifying as gender fluid, gender free, bi-gender or non-binary.

Some young people begin to live part time in their affirmed gender, some beginning their transition only within environments that they deem safe, easing into or testing out their transition. Breaking down the transition into more digestible chunks can help prepare the young T/GE person for a fuller social transition that will assist them emotionally, mentally and socially.

Living more full time in their affirmed gender involves coming out more broadly at school, in communities, and having teachers and other adults begin to use their affirmed name and personal gender pronouns. Social transitioning in a child welfare setting—a group home, congregate care setting or foster home—may pose some challenges, but policies and practices, rather than personal attitudes of the professional staff, should guide the process and always focus on the best interest of the young person.

There have been studies to suggest that T/GE youth who are able to live in their affirmed gender in the world may have less significant levels of depression and anxiety, and overall possess less risk of mental health problems (Hill & Menvielle, 2009; Hill *et al.*, 2010; Kuvalanka, Weiner & Mahan, 2014; Olson *et al.*, 2016; Simons *et al.*, 2013). Sawyer affirms this suggestion:

> When I was not able to be myself, I was so miserable. I remember trying to convince people that I was a girl. But that was so tiring and depressing. I was on medication, hospitalized twice for trying to commit suicide. Once I worked with my therapist and I started to transition, first I kinda lived half in and half out, but then I just came all the way out and lived full time as Sawyer. Once I was completely out living full time as I always wanted to be, my life changed so much.

I still have good days and bad days, but I am off medication, I haven't been hospitalized in five years and I feel like the person I was always meant to be. What a relief it is to be able to be yourself.

Medical transition

It is important to note that not all T/GE youth will choose to pursue a "medical transition." There are numerous factors that go into this decision-making: socio-economic status, the strength of the individual T/GE young person's gender dysphoria and the presence of other health conditions (American Public Health Association, 2016).

Gender fluid or non-binary youth may decide not to pursue a medical transition, or they may choose to pursue some of the medical interventions. Some of these young people may choose some surgery, but no hormones; others will choose hormones, but no surgery.

Professional staff should be able to assist those T/GE youth people who choose to pursue medical interventions by familiarizing themselves with the Standards of Care Guidelines.

Using World Professional Association for Transgender Health (WPATH) Standards of Care (SOC) as flexible guidelines

WPATH is an international multi-disciplinary professional association with a mission to promote evidence-based practice, care, education, research, advocacy and public policy with respect to T/GE health and mental health care. Although these Standards of Care (Coleman *et al.*, 2011) are primarily written for adults, Chapter VI, Assessment and Treatment of Children and Adolescents with Gender Dysphoria, focuses on medical and mental health treatment approaches for T/GE children and youth. The full document is available online[2] for free and provides clinical guidance for health care professionals to assist T/GE people with "safe and effective pathways to achieving lasting personal comfort with their gendered selves, in order to maximize their overall health, psychological well-being, and self-fulfillment" (Coleman *et al.*,

---

2   www.wpath.org

2012, p.1). In addition to describing the role of mental health providers, which we discussed in the previous chapter, the Standards of Care provide guidelines for making decisions regarding medical transitions related to hormone and surgical treatments.

Although some health care providers have interpreted these Standards of Care literally, the authors intended the standards to be flexible so that they can better meet the diverse needs of T/GE people (Johnson & Wassersug, 2016). In this way, the standards are meant to be modified by health care providers and adapted in various cultural contexts as well. Chang and colleagues (2018, p.144) urge that practitioners refrain from using the standards as a "rigid resource to be applied in the same way for all T/GE clients." These experienced clinical practitioners also point out that:

> Although there is debate about the appropriateness of the WPATH SOC, as a clinician, it is important for you to familiarize yourself with the standards and to stay current with the changes in the WPATH's recommendations and T/GE health. Many health care systems and insurance companies follow the WPATH Standards of Care, so regardless of your stance, it is important to be informed about current requirements that are affecting your client's access to care. (Chang *et al.*, 2018, p.145)

There are some universal components referring to specific medical interventions and, in general, the Standards of Care indicate that:

- a diagnosis of persistent, well-documented gender dysphoria is required

- capacity to make fully informed decisions and to consent to treatment is necessary

- if youth are not of the age of majority, clinicians are advised to follow the standards outlined for the section titled Assessment and Treatment of Children and Adolescents with Gender Dysphoria and parental consent is required, although this may vary from locality to locality

- if significant medical or mental health concerns are present, they must be reasonably well controlled. (Coleman *et al.*, 2012)

Medical interventions for T/GE youth

The medical interventions that are available to assist T/GE youth with gender transition can include one or more of the following in these two broad categories:

- Hormone therapy

- Gender-affirming surgeries.

Hormone therapy

Some, but not all, T/GE young people wish to or choose to undergo hormone therapy (Clark, Marshall & Saewyc, 2020). Hormone therapy can be categorized into two broad areas for young people: puberty blockers and feminizing and masculinizing hormone therapy. Hormone therapy depends on the young person's goals, and can range from brief periods of treatment to lifelong continual use. Hormones may have physical and emotional effects for the young person using them. This section provides an overview of hormone therapy including puberty blockers and masculinizing and feminizing hormone therapy for young T/GE men and T/GE women.

Puberty blockers

With T/GE children, hormone blockers are typically prescribed in the initial stages of puberty or peri-pubescent youth. Puberty blockers are medications that delay the onset of puberty or halt the progress of puberty.[3] Although there are interventions related to social transition for this age group, due to age limitations, there are no medical interventions for T/GE youth prior to the onset of puberty. Puberty blockers are most effective when they are started immediately after the onset of puberty. Having a prescription for puberty blockers allows a young person more time to gain clarity about their gender identity without going through puberty developments. The start of puberty in T/GE children often brings about an increased sense of body dysphoria and can potentially create another set of comorbidities, including depression, anxiety, substance use and possible suicidal ideation or gestures. If puberty blockers are discontinued, the young person's body

---

3   www.seattlechildrens.org/pdf/PE2572.pdf

will proceed with its biological development. If puberty blockers are started late in puberty, they cannot reverse most changes that have already happened. However, they can stop any further puberty changes.

These medications can only be prescribed by a physician, preferably a pediatric endocrinologist who has greater knowledge and expertise about adolescents and their hormonal well-being (Hembree *et al.*, 2017). Puberty blockers prevent the development of secondary sexual characteristics (breast budding and the onset of menses in cisgender females; the increase in testicular volume and scrotal skin and facial hair in cisgender males; and the growth of pubic hair in both males and females) that match the young person's designated gender rather than their affirmed gender. There are several advantages in using puberty blockers with pre-pubescent T/GE youth. By suspending the development of secondary sexual characteristics that match the young person's designated gender at birth and then moving directly to masculinizing or feminizing hormones, there is no need to reverse or undo the effects of the secondary sexual characteristics. Another benefit is that the use of puberty blockers and the cessation of secondary sexual characteristics can bring about a significant reduction in gender dysphoria and, as such, can diminish the profound distress that many T/GE youth feel when their body does not match their internal sense of gender identity. But not all T/GE youth come out early enough to start puberty blockers.

The requirements for T/GE youth to begin puberty-blocking medications are outlined in the WPATH guidelines and include the following criteria:

- A long-lasting and intense pattern of gender variance or dysphoria has been demonstrated.

- Gender dysphoria has emerged or worsened with the onset of puberty.

- Any co-existing psychological, medical or social problems have been sufficiently stabilized so they will not likely interfere with treatment.

- Informed consent has been obtained from the youth or the parent/guardian if the youth is younger than the age of medical consent, and parents/guardians are willing to support the youth during the treatment process. (Coleman *et al.*, 2012)

Some physicians require a written mental health assessment supporting this intervention; others do not, as the effects of the medication are reversible. However, most youth who undergo puberty blocker treatment then go on to begin feminizing or masculinizing hormone therapy, which is explored in the next section.

There are two types of puberty-blocking medications which have been used:

- *Lupron Depot* or *Leuprolide:* Given as an injection (shot) once every three months, administered in a physician's office.

- *Histrelin:* A small plastic rod is placed under the skin in the upper arm. The implant works for approximately one year, but can last up to two years or longer. After it stops working, it will need to be removed and replaced by a physician.

The long-term safety of puberty-blocking medicines is not completely understood (De Vries *et al.*, 2014) and there may be risks that we do not know about yet.[4]

There are three areas that may cause concern and require further discussion with parents/caregivers and health care providers:

Bone health: Blocking puberty can make bones weaker (lower bone density). While on puberty blockers, it is recommended that young people take calcium and vitamin D and do bone strength-building exercises like walking, jumping and weight-lifting. Bone health should be checked by a physician every two years while they are on blockers.

Fertility: Taking puberty blockers should not affect a person's ability to have a child in the future; however, permanent damage to fertility is a concern for those who stay on puberty blockers and then take masculinizing/feminizing hormone therapy. It is recommended that young people talk about this with a physician to fully understand the potential impact on fertility before starting any medicines.

---

4   www.stlouischildrens.org/conditions-treatments/transgender-center/puberty-blockers

Cost: Puberty blockers can be expensive. Some insurance companies cover them, some do not. How much insurance covers depends on the insurance plan and requires authorization from the plan. Sometimes insurance companies will only help pay for Lupron Depot and not Histrelin (Nahata *et al.*, 2017).

Puberty blockers can be used until the T/GE young person decides either to resume the puberty process, or is ready to start masculinizing or feminizing hormones. Because puberty blockers can make bones weaker over time, it is best to discontinue them after about four years.

Starting puberty blockers can give a young T/GE person time before making more permanent gender decisions, like starting masculinizing or feminizing hormones. The dysphoric body distress that some T/GE young people experience can be somewhat alleviated by pushing the "pause button" on puberty, which will prevent puberty changes that do not match the T/GE young person's gender identity. For some people, puberty blockers may reduce the need for future gender-affirming surgeries or other treatments such as breast removal (mastectomies) for T/GE men, or hair removal and breast surgery for T/GE women.

Feminizing and masculinizing hormone therapy

Given that feminizing and masculinizing hormone therapies are irreversible, these interventions should begin when the T/GE young person is firmly grounded in their affirmed gender. Ideally, this decision should be made collaboratively between the young person, their family and their health care provider (Bauer *et al.*, 2009).

Feminizing hormone therapy

T/GE women designated male at birth may seek feminizing hormone therapy. Those who make this choice will be prescribed two types of medications: *estrogen* and an *anti-androgen*—sometimes called a testosterone or androgen blocker. Androgen blockers suppress the effects of testosterone on the body. Most hormones are administered orally, or via a skin patch, but some are given by injection. The physical changes that can result from these hormones include softer skin, changes in body hair, breast development, redistribution of body fat and decreased muscle mass and tone. Some things will not change: facial hair will not completely disappear (and some young people may require electrolysis or laser hair removal); the Adam's apple may not decrease in size; facial bone structure will remain the same as before the administration of the medication; and the pitch of the voice will not change.

T/GE young people without financial resources who may not be able to afford hormone therapy sometimes access hormones on the streets or online. The dosage and purity of these medications are not assured and increases the risks to the young person. In some cases, young people share needles and may inject with others, creating additional health risks. Similarly, injecting silicon into one's breasts from a non-medical source can cause disfigurement and health complications.

Masculinizing hormone therapy

T/GE men designated female at birth may seek masculinizing hormone therapy. Those who make this choice will be prescribed testosterone. This is most frequently given in the form of an intramuscular injection, but it can also be administered with topical gels or creams or a dermal patch. The dosage depends on the young person's goals; some start with a lower dose to have a gradual masculinizing process or to support a more androgynous appearance. Encouraging young people to adhere to the prescribed dosage is important as taking higher levels of testosterone than prescribed can mean that the testosterone is converted to estrogen, which would actually inhibit the masculinization process. Typically, the results from this type of therapy include facial and body hair growth, increased male pattern baldness, deepening of the voice and enlarged clitoral tissue. Other changes include the cessation of menses, changes in body fat distribution, increased muscle mass and tone, increased sex drive and changes to the vaginal lining or secretions. It is important to note that testosterone is not an adequate form of birth control—the cessation of menses does not preclude an ability to become pregnant. Transmen who do not have a hysterectomy have their fertility options intact.

The WPATH Standards of Care indicate that adolescents may initiate the feminization or masculinization therapies at the age of 16.

Some physicians will categorically not prescribe feminization or masculinization therapies for T/GE youth younger than 18. For the initiation of feminization or masculinizing hormone therapy some health care systems require a letter from a mental health professional, which is consistent with the Standards of Care from WPATH, but others may utilize an informed consent model and thus bypass the mental health assessment.

The use of hormone therapy has risks. Testosterone can damage the liver, especially if taken in high doses or by mouth. Estrogen can increase blood pressure, blood glucose (sugar) and blood clotting. Anti-androgens, such as spironolactone, can lower blood pressure, disturb electrolytes and dehydrate the body. Hormone use should always be supervised by a doctor. Young people who smoke, drink excessively or have a mental health condition should be carefully monitored for any possible side effects of the medications that can be exacerbated due to these factors. In summary, T/GE people who are given masculinizing or feminizing hormones should only do so under the supervision of a doctor, preferably an endocrinologist, who can prescribe an appropriate dose and monitor its effects.

Gender-affirming surgery

This section provides an overview of the various types of gender-affirming surgery procedures. It is important to note that not all T/GE young people opt to have this kind of surgery. T/GE youth who desire gender-affirming surgeries may choose to have some surgeries and not others.

Chang and colleagues (2018) urge practitioners to discuss with young people a range of topics regarding surgical interventions, including:

- *expectations* they may have about the surgery

- *emotional preparation*—the emotions associated with this significant life event

- *coping and relaxation skills assessment*—to deal with the physical and emotional stress that they will undoubtedly encounter

- *financial planning and concerns*—not only about the payment for these procedures, but about taking time off from school or work and the financial burden that this might involve

- *medical stability*—possible concerns could include cardiac health, response to anesthesia, weight (and body mass index—BMI) and substance abuse issues

- *recovery and logistics*—young people will need a well-thought-out and solid plan for aftercare and reliable support.

The question about whether to have genital surgery is a highly personal and intrusive one. The implication is that the questioner wants to know whether the person is a "real" man or woman. However, given the costs and the insurance implications of surgery, and the safety aspects and the ability to change one's identification documents, there are complex issues for T/GE people to consider.

Also, important to note is that, for T/GE youth, the more recent terms for genital surgery are "gender-affirming" and "gender-confirming" surgery. Previous terms that included words like "redesignated" are negated by using these terms, which instead focus on the gender in which one is affirmed or confirmed via medical procedures.

Surgical interventions for T/GE feminine young people

People on the T/GE feminine spectrum may be interested in a number of surgical interventions including chest reconstruction, genital reconstruction, facial feminization and vocal cord surgeries.

Chest reconstruction surgeries are sometimes referred to as "top surgeries." Top surgery for transfeminine women includes breast augmentation using silicone or saline implants. This is not cosmetic, but medically necessary in reducing gender dysphoria, and can increase safety. Being seen in one's affirmed gender is one of the most critical factors that determines whether a young transfeminine person is free from verbal harassment or physical violence in private or public settings. For T/GE youth who may have experienced years of being misgendered, this surgery contributes to their ability to have others in the world see and acknowledge them in their affirmed gender (Ansara & Hegarty, 2012). For many, having visible breasts is a primary way for someone to be perceived as female.

As with hormone therapy, top surgery requires a letter[5] from the young person's doctor. There is no specific timetable associated with this procedure, and decisions should be flexible and individualized according to the young person's needs, and the risks and benefits for them. Some physicians may be reluctant to perform top surgery before a young person reaches the age of 18 years, but for T/GE youth who have transitioned earlier and whose gender has remained consistent, there are some physicians who will perform the surgery at 16 or 17 years of age. Parental consent is required for all surgical procedures for minors.

Genital reconstructive surgeries for transfeminine women will typically have two options: orchiectomy and vaginoplasty. The term "bottom" surgery is often used by T/GE people informally to denote these surgeries. An orchiectomy is the removal of the testes from the scrotum. This reduces testosterone production, which can be helpful in alleviating gender dysphoria for some transfeminine women.

A vaginoplasty is a surgical procedure that involves rearranging the current tissue, and/or extra tissue from other parts of the body, in the genital area to create the vaginal canal and external genitalia, the labia. To create the vaginal canal, the surgeon uses the skin surrounding the existing penis in addition to the scrotal skin.

The clitoris is constructed using tissue from the glans penis. When the surgery is performed by a skilled and knowledgeable surgeon, the appearance of the vagina post-surgery is no different from a cisgender woman's vagina.

In large part, due to the costs of these procedures and whether or not they may be reimbursed by insurance, some transfeminine women choose to have the orchiectomy rather than the vaginoplasty.

Ariel provides this detailed account of her gender-affirming surgery. Her honesty and directness may be instrumental in helping professionals understand what this experience entails without having to ask a young person to provide details of their own surgery:

Obviously, getting a vagina was incredible, but I couldn't appreciate it at the time, because right after the surgery it looked really messed up.

---

5   For a sample letter see https://transline.zendesk.com/hc/en-us/articles/229372788-Surgery-Sample-Letter

After they took out all of the packing, I could start dilating. And to be honest, dilating at first was really, really difficult for me. It wasn't the most painful thing in the world, it just felt very, very bizarre to put a plastic dildo in a hole that had never existed—it felt so foreign, and I was just really scared of that feeling. That really messed me up for the first day, and I was really emotional. It is a painful experience and it is also very emotionally exhausting. You don't really appreciate getting a vagina when you are in constant pain and when it is all messed up.

And then you go home and you have to dilate four times a day for the first month, and then it goes down to three times a day for the next two months and then twice a day after that. I stopped feeling pain down there about a month and a half after surgery. It does get easier and the pain does go away.

Eleven weeks after surgery I lost my virginity and it felt great, it didn't hurt—it was great. I have been told that my vagina looks very nice. It is quite tight, from what I have heard from the people that have been in there. It looks very natural. There is a lot of sensation on my clit and it feels great on the inside too. My scars are visible, but they are not so bad and blend into my skin tone. I highly recommend getting hair removal before the surgery, because, if you don't, you can get hairs growing inside your vagina and that is something that you do not want.

Additional medical procedures which may be sought by some transfeminine women include a tracheal shave to reduce the size of the Adam's apple, and removal of body hair by electrolysis or laser treatments. Some transfeminine women also opt for surgical procedures for voice feminization, although many have voice coaching to enhance pitch and tone rather than surgery.

The WPATH Standards of Care require two letters from mental health professionals for these surgeries.[6] Additionally, the individual should have lived in the gender role that is congruent with their affirmed gender identity and, if they have been prescribed hormones, they should have completed one year of hormone therapy.

---

6 For samples of letters which mental health providers can use see https://transline.zendesk.com/hc/en-us/articles/229372788-Surgery-Sample-Letter

Surgical interventions for T/GE masculine young people

Young people on the T/GE masculine spectrum may be interested in a number of surgical options, including chest reconstructive surgery, hysterectomy, and oophorectomy and genital reconstructive surgeries such as metoidioplasty and phalloplasty.

Chest reconstruction surgeries are sometimes referred to as "top surgeries" and there are several options. These surgeries change the contour and appearance of a person's chest. Some people have a desire to have a chest that is more stereotypically masculine in appearance, while others pursue this surgery to have a flat or neutral chest. There are two main options for this surgery: "double incision" and "key hole" surgery. In the first, as the name implies, two incisions are made, excess skin is removed and the nipple is removed and then reattached. In the key hole surgery, excess tissue is removed via liposuction.

It is important to note that in the past it has been believed that only T/GE masculine individuals wished to have this surgery, but increasingly more gender-variant people, who may not identify as trans, are also seeking some forms of top surgery.

The WPATH Standards of Care require one letter from mental health professionals as recommendation for these surgeries.[7] Additionally, the individual should have lived in the gender role that is congruent with their affirmed gender identity, and if they have been prescribed hormones, they should have completed one year of hormone therapy.

Some T/GE people, motivated by reducing their gender dysphoria, bringing about the cessation of menses, eliminating the need for gynecological care or reducing hormone therapy, may opt for a hysterectomy (removal of the uterus, cervix and fallopian tubes) and oophorectomy (removal of the ovaries). These procedures were once believed to be necessary for cancer prevention, but as Chang and colleagues (2018) note in citing Asscheman *et al.*'s (2011) study, this claim has not been validated. However, some T/GE people desire this surgery because having organs that are associated with being designated female brings up dysphoria and discomfort.

---

7   For a sample letter see www.thegenderhealthcenter.org/resources/providers/ SAMPLE-FTM_Top_Surgery_Clearance_Letter.pdf

The WPATH Standards of Care require two letters from mental health professionals as recommendation for these surgeries.

Genital reconstructive surgeries for transmasculine young people
Metoidioplasty and phalloplasty are two options available to T/GE masculine young people. Metoidioplasty, sometimes called "meta," involves "releasing" the clitoris, which has become enlarged as a result of testosterone therapy. The procedure creates a small phallus and can be done without the urethral lengthening which allows the individual to urinate while standing up.

During a phalloplasty, physicians remove a flap of skin from a donor area of the body. This tissue is used to make both the urethra and the shaft of the penis, in a tube-within-a-tube structure. The larger tube is basically rolled around the inside tube. Skin grafts are then taken from inconspicuous areas of the body, where they will leave no visible scars, and grafted on to the donation site. Since the female urethra is shorter than the male urethra, surgeons can lengthen the urethra and attach it to the female urethra so that urine will flow from the tip of the penis. The clitoris is usually left in place near the base of the penis, where it can still be stimulated. Phalloplasty is really a series of surgeries performed in stages; in addition to the grafting process, a penile implant, which involves additional surgery, can be inserted into the phallus allowing for penetrative sex. Cost, lack of insurance coverage, unrealistic appearance and minimal sensations are some of the reasons that not all T/GE masculine individuals pursue this "bottom" surgery. However, recent advances which have improved the appearance, sexual satisfaction, pleasure and post-surgical complications also make these surgeries more gratifying for some young T/GE people. Young people and their families will need to have accurate information and open discussions about the range of options available to them, and opportunities to correct misconceptions.

Like Ariel in the previous narrative, Lee provides this open and honest account of their experience with gender-affirming surgery:

There is not so much information out there about testosterone and getting top surgery, but in comparison, there is very little information out there about getting a penis. I had a metoidioplasty. This basically creates a micro-penis from your existing clit—nothing is added apart from silicon balls, if that's what you want, and I do have them.

Before I did this surgery, I did extensive research. I did so much reading, but I feel like I still went into this not knowing everything I needed to know about lower and bottom surgery—and I didn't know everything that was gonna happen—all the little details—and there were quite a few surprises.

There were many years between top surgery and bottom surgery for me, in part because I just didn't know what was what when it came to bottom surgery. I had a few complications, and they haven't affected my results. I am very happy with the outcome. It was definitely the right thing for me to do.

Getting bottom surgery is really private and very sensitive. The results are less instant than top surgery—your body needs time to heal and may need revisions. There can be lots of bruising and the final size of your penis may take time too. I had a lot of swelling and it was bigger at first, but then when everything calmed down and I healed, it was smaller. Every bit of going to the bathroom after bottom surgery is more difficult at first. To be honest, it takes a bit of getting used to after you have had your whole genital area reconfigured. I mean it's all changed quite extensively, even if this is what you really, really wanted. You have gone from nothing sticking out there, to stuff sticking out and sometimes it gets in the way. I am still getting used to the balls. I mean the fact that when I sit, I can feel them—that's very weird. It doesn't mean I am unhappy. I just mean my body has changed quite a bit and it takes some getting used to.

The WPATH Standards of Care require two letters from mental health professionals for these surgeries. Additionally, the individual should have lived in the gender role that is congruent with their affirmed gender identity for a minimum of one year, and have had one year of hormone therapy. The primary goal underlying these considerations within the Standards of Care is to ensure that the T/GE youth has had the opportunity to experience living in their affirmed gender both internally and socially prior to making decisions involving irreversible physical changes.

Even though the Standards of Care indicate that gender-affirming surgeries should only be performed after the age of consent as an adult, it is important for professionals to be knowledgeable about these procedures when working with T/GE youth. Young people and their families will often want to know what options are available for them as the young person moves into adulthood. For a more detailed discussion and description of these gender-affirming surgeries, see Chang, Singh and dickey's (2018, pp.152–159) text.

Conclusion

Identifying trans-competent health and mental health care providers is a critical step in the process of social and medical transition. While some physicians may have knowledge about the protocols associated with hormone therapy and puberty blockers, others may have little to no knowledge and may be unwilling to provide hormone treatment for a T/GE adolescent. Location can also play a key role in determining access to trans-affirming care (Deutsch, 2016). The ability to cover the financial costs of these procedures and/or the lack of health care coverage can also limit a T/GE youth's ability to medically transition.

Youth care workers and mental health professionals play important roles in working with a young person and their family to identify health care and mental health care providers with knowledge and skill to provide the types of services that they may need. T/GE youth have health-related concerns that are unique to their status and they will need trans-affirming health and mental health care providers.

To find a trans-affirming therapist there are a few places people may search online.[8] Psychology Today[9] is a public site for mental health care where information can be found using key terms such as "transgender."

The health care options associated with gender-affirming transition have too often been misunderstood as cosmetic, experimental or simply unnecessary. Yet there is medical consensus that hormone therapy and gender-affirming surgery are medically necessary for many T/GE people. It's quite clear now that a person's gender identity—one's inner

---

8   www.transcaresite.org
9   www.psychologytoday.com

sense of being male or female—is deep-seated and cannot be changed. Therefore, this transition-related health care can be crucial.

To find out how to access hormone therapy, it's essential for a person, if they have insurance, to reach out to their individual insurance carrier to inquire about their personal coverage. The first step is to call the member services' phone number listed on the insurance card to ask about coverage for the specific services they need. They have a right to request a copy of their policy that covers any trans/gender-affirmation medical treatments. They may want to take the information they learn or a copy of the policy with them when they see their current physician to talk about what it means for access to care.

There are many physicians who perform gender-affirming surgeries and it's possible to search for these online.[10] Some people check online with others who are in surgery groups for T/GE and non-binary people,[11] where they can see photographs and talk with people who have worked with a particular surgeon. When there is more than one option to choose from, it is important to learn as much as possible about a potential surgeon before making a final choice. Sometimes there may be only one option available. It is important to ask about what insurance coverage a surgeon accepts for payment, if any, before decisions are made on who to pursue surgery with.

In this chapter, we discussed the gender-affirming medical interventions of hormone therapy and gender-affirming surgeries for transmasculine and transfeminine individuals and some key areas that professionals should discuss with T/GE youth with whom they are working. As this information was a brief overview of these complex topics, it is critical that professionals seek consultation and training from experienced health care providers. The discussion and recommendations provided here solely serve as a foundation of basic practice knowledge for providers working with T/GE youth.

---

10 www.transcaresite.org

11 Such as www.transbucket.com

CHAPTER 4

Educational Issues

School and school-related activities comprise a major portion of a young person's life. T/GE students, including non-binary youth, must cope with unique stresses that their cisgender and lesbian, gay and bisexual counterparts do not have to face in school settings. These stresses, especially regarding safety (Allen *et al.*, 2020), which are related in large part to their identities as T/GE individuals, may interfere with school socialization, school success and the educational process itself. T/GE young people are often subject to verbal taunts and harassment directly altogether.

Lee's narrative below illustrates the difficulties that some T/GE youth face in school settings:

> School was a living hell for me. I began to socially transition in the tenth grade. If I had to do it again, I probably would have done it in the ninth grade when I started the new school, but I just wasn't ready at that time. Oh my God, changing my name and my pronoun was like the biggest thing that ever happened in this school. Most of the teachers, except for the gym teachers, were pretty cool with my transition, but a lot of the kids were fucking horrible. It wore me out. I got so exhausted from trying to watch my back and deal with all the verbal insults that were hurled at me. I finally couldn't take it anymore and I just never went back. I took the GED [General Education Development tests] and passed, and that was the end of my high school career. It wasn't that I didn't like school—I just couldn't take the abuse anymore.

Anyone who has been a teenager, which is everyone, can recall the ups and downs of high school. In spite of the challenges, schools are important places for young people. The following statistics suggest a reality of school systems for T/GE young people that is different from the experiences of their cisgender or lesbian, gay and bisexual peers. A national survey by the Gay, Lesbian, Straight Educators Network (GLSEN) found the following:

- 85 percent of T/GE students were harassed or assaulted at school because of their gender.

- 83 percent of T/GE students felt unsafe at school because of their gender.

- 80 percent of T/GE students said they'd avoided bathrooms because they felt unsafe or uncomfortable.

- 64 percent of T/GE students avoided gym classes because they felt unsafe or uncomfortable.

- 59 percent of T/GE students had been required to use a bathroom that did not match the gender they lived every day.

- 51 percent of T/GE students were unable to use the name or pronoun that matched their gender.

- 25 percent of T/GE students had been prevented from wearing clothes because they were considered inappropriate based on legal sex.

- 12 percent of T/GE and gender-diverse students reported that their school or district had official policies or guidelines supporting T/GE students. (Kosciw *et al.*, 2018)

In addition to these troublesome statistics, too often school officials themselves single out these youth by refusing to respect their gender identity or expression and even punishing them for expressing that identity. For example, 80 percent of T/GE students have been denied access to restrooms consistent with their gender identity. Rather than focusing on their education, many students struggle to come to school and be themselves without being punished for wearing clothes or using facilities consistent with who they are. Some are denied opportunities to go on field trips or participate in sports. Together with bullying and victim-blaming, these conflicts can lead to disproportionate discipline, school pushouts and, in some cases, involvement in the juvenile justice system. Conversely, T/GE students in schools with supportive policies are less likely to miss school because they feel unsafe, and have a greater sense of belonging to their school communities.

This chapter addresses educational issues for T/GE youth. It begins with a discussion about the ways in which schools can explore the social transition process for these young people, focusing primarily on how school systems can develop a trans-positive environment for teachers, school personnel and students. This is followed by descriptions of best practices to create, support and maintain inclusive environments for T/GE and all youth in school systems.

Coming out at school

When a young person decides to socially transition, it is important to remember that the student is undergoing a uniquely individual and personal experience; even though many young people like attention, few youth want to be the center of attention, particularly for such a personal matter. By considering the issues proactively, parents and caregivers, youth workers, educators and school officials can help protect the student's right to feel safe from others' comments, questions and rumors and allow the student to preserve their dignity and privacy. In many schools, while there might be some genuinely innocent confusion or uncertainty from teachers, staff and students that may arise as a T/GE youth socially transitions, it is the school administration's responsibility to set clear boundaries about what is and is not appropriate to say to the student or their family.

Nealy (2019) suggests that it can be helpful to begin a social transition at school on the first day back from a break, or in September at the start of the school year. Creating a fresh start with new teachers and new students, where the young person can be met in their affirmed gender using their affirmed name and personal gender pronouns, can ease some of the challenges of a social transition as opposed to transitioning in mid-year. But the young person's decision about when to transition may not always match the academic timetable. The timing of the young person's social transition in school is a decision that they should make in collaboration with their family and in discussion with school personnel.

Striking a balance in providing education about gender diversity in general while still respecting the student's right to and need for privacy is critical in maintaining confidentiality. As evidenced by Petra's narrative below, schools that have had the foresight to work to be more gender inclusive when a student transitions will promote greater understanding and acceptance.

> My school was pretty good when I transitioned in the ninth grade. I was new to the school, so I came in as Petra, and the teachers, staff and students were all very positive about me. The school had done training on gender issues, the bathrooms were gender neutral and the students seemed to act like it was not a big deal. It was the first time I could actually relax and focus on my schoolwork rather than worry about what bathroom I was gonna use.

Schools must also be able to respond to negative reactions to a student's gender transition. Schools are obligated legally and ethically to serve as a buffer to protect students and their families. Without speaking about the specific student, educators, administrators and other school staff can use these talking points, as suggested by Orr and colleagues (2015, p.17), to respond to questions or negative reactions from the school community:

> "I know this is new territory for many of us. Sometimes change is really challenging. Perhaps I can share some information with you about gender identity and T/GE people?"

> "I can assure you that the safety, well-being and education of all students remain our highest priorities."

> "Of course, I can't talk about any individual student, just as I would never talk about your child."

> "Schools have always worked to support the needs of individual students in a variety of ways. Like we have always done, we are committed to supporting all of our students."

"Imagine if this was another type of student need that other people weren't comfortable with, how would you respond?"

Negative reactions frequently stem from a lack of knowledge of or familiarity with the reality of T/GE people. Regardless of any one person's discomfort, T/GE students who are socially transitioning in school need to be safe and supported. There may even be some parents/caregivers who oppose the school's decision to support and affirm T/GE students and may attempt to involve local media to pressure the school and district to reverse their actions. The school or district can choose whether or not to respond to media inquiries, but should always keep in mind the issues of confidentiality for the student who is transitioning. Schools or districts should not discourage T/GE students or their families from a transition simply because it requires additional contingency planning. Regardless of whether a student's social transition is public or private, it is the school's or district's obligation to be prepared for a variety of circumstances that could occur. The ongoing process for supporting a T/GE student throughout their social transition must be central to the school's strategy.

Meeting with the school

A young person's social transition at school, whether it is at the beginning of an academic year or mid-year, needs to start with a meeting between parents or caregivers, the young person and the school. It might be best to begin the conversation with the young person's guidance counselor or an assistant principal. The initial focus of the meeting should be the disclosure of the young person's affirmed gender identity and the intent to have the young person recognized by their affirmed name and personal gender pronouns. How this should be announced and what accommodations should be made should be addressed at this time as well. Parents and caregivers should be prepared to take some printed information to the meeting, or send it beforehand.

When schools have previously addressed gender identity issues, the assumption is that the staff will have a basic knowledge about these issues, but in some cases, this knowledge may not be as detailed as necessary for having an out T/GE student in their school setting.

Parents and caregivers should inquire about the school's previous experiences of working with T/GE students and ask for copies of the school's written policies and guidelines. If this is the first time that the school system has addressed these issues then parents and caregivers should be prepared to provide resources to the school personnel and advocate for policies or accommodations.

The Department of Education (DOE)/Department of Justice (DOJ) letter of 2016 from the Obama administration explicitly stated that T/GE students did not need to produce a medical diagnosis or birth certificate; instead, a parent or guardian's assertion that the student's gender identity differed from previous records or representations was sufficient for the school to be required to recognize that student's affirmed gender. This directive was rescinded by the repressive Trump administration, stating that the earlier directive needed to be withdrawn because it lacked extensive legal analysis, did not go through a public vetting process, sowed confusion and drew legal challenges. The administration further directed that schools "treat a student's gender identity as the student's sex for purposes of Title IX and its implementing regulation" (Human Rights Campaign, 2020, p.6).

The Obama administration's guidelines had provided much-needed clarification on T/GE protections. By rescinding the guidance, the Trump administration sent a deeply troubling message to students that it would not stand up for students' civil rights. Despite the Department of Education's latest repressive actions, individual school districts remain free to voluntarily allow T/GE students to access the bathroom matching their gender identity.

As such, many schools are back to asking for parents and caregivers to provide a letter from the young person's medical doctor or mental health provider attesting to the young person's diagnosis of gender dysphoria.

In maintaining good practice with T/GE students, schools should, however, continue to avoid requiring medical, legal or other "proof" in order to respect a student's gender identity. The decision to undergo a particular medical treatment as part of a transition is a very personal one that must be left to the student, their family and their health care provider. In addition to being overly invasive, such a requirement for proof does not account for the many barriers T/GE youth experience when trying to access transition-related medical care (Gridley *et al.*, 2016; Stotzer, Silverschanz & Wilson, 2013). It is similarly inappropriate to require specific court orders or changes to government-issued identity documents. Additionally, some students do not want or need medical care. Due to varying state and federal policies, T/GE youth very often are unable to change government-issued identity documents and other records to correspond to their chosen name and appropriate gender (Russell *et al.*, 2018; Sequeira *et al.*, 2019). In fact, some states do not allow correction of gender markers at all, and many allow individuals to change their gender marker on identity documents only on completion of medical procedures that are unavailable to young people. Schools have found that in practice it is not difficult to verify that a student is really T/GE, regardless of whether they can present medical or legal evidence. In rare cases where a school administrator suspects that a student is initiating a formal process to discuss a transition for an improper purpose, the administrator can seek additional clarification about the student's needs and objectives.

Creating a safe and inclusive environment at school

There are several key areas where the school will need to address issues specific to the transition of a T/GE youth.

Record keeping

A school's record-keeping and reporting requirements are often viewed as a challenging barrier to overcome. In spite of this, many school districts have found solutions that allow them to comply with state and local requirements while meeting their obligations to safeguard a T/GE student's privacy and right to learn in a safe and supportive school environment. Orr and colleagues (2015, p.22) offer the following examples of these solutions, but their viability in any school depends on a variety of factors, including each state's legal requirements for record keeping and student information systems.

- Maintain a copy of the student's birth certificate or other identity document that reflects the student's name and sex as designated at birth under lock and key in the principal's office, while the student information system has the name and gender marker that correspond to the student's gender identity.

- Allow the student to re-enroll in the school using a passport with the correct name and gender marker, or change the name and gender marker in the student information system to be consistent with the passport. If a student is a US citizen and their family can afford the passport application fees, obtaining a passport that reflects the student's gender identity is usually easier than changing that information on their birth certificate.

- Use the student's chosen name and gender in the student information system, but switch it to the student's legal name and gender just before uploading the information to the state department of education's database. Schools that choose this approach pull that student's testing booklet before it is distributed and correct the name and gender marker on the label to ensure that the student's privacy and identity are respected.

- Create a uniform and public procedure at the district level that connects all electronic student databases and allows a student or their parent to fill out one form indicating the name and personal gender pronoun the student wishes to use. Some school districts have established such procedures to streamline the process and reduce the common bureaucratic barriers.

- Work with the student information system provider to develop a field or screen that would allow the district to maintain the student's legal and chosen name, but that would use the chosen name to populate attendance sheets, report cards, and other school-related documents.

Names and personal gender pronouns

An individual's name and personal gender pronouns are an important part of that person's identity. In many ways, they define how someone is perceived and affect how they interact with others. Consistently using a T/GE student's chosen name and personal gender pronouns signals that the person is respecting and affirming the T/GE student's gender identity. Using the student's chosen name and personal gender pronoun models and sets expectations for the school community. Conversely, intentionally using a T/GE student's prior name and associated personal gender pronouns will make that student feel unsafe and unwelcome, and will interfere with their ability to learn. While this book focuses primarily on T/GE youth who are transitioning from male to female or female to male, it is important to note that a growing number of gender-expansive youth identify outside the gender binary, and many use gender-neutral personal gender pronouns. Although it may be more difficult for some child welfare and education professionals to adapt to gender-neutral pronouns, it is still important to do so in support of the student.

Changing identity documents can be cumbersome, and schools may use a young person's affirmed name and personal gender pronoun even if there has been no legal name change. The high cost of obtaining a court-ordered name change in states that require transition-related surgery before correcting the gender marker on a birth certificate prevents students from obtaining identity documents that reflect their true selves. Consequently, school and district personnel must develop policies and protocols for inputting the correct information into the student information system regardless of the student's legal name or gender marker.

Dress codes

T/GE students should have the right to dress in a manner consistent with their gender identity or gender expression as long as the student's attire complies with the school- or district-wide dress code. If the school or district has a specific dress code for boys and girls, a T/GE student must be allowed to wear the clothing that corresponds to their gender identity, regardless of their designated sex at birth, the gender designated on their birth certificate or other legal documents.

Sex-separated facilities, activities and programs

Another crucial element in supporting a transitioning student is giving them access to sex-separated facilities, activities or programs based on the student's gender identity. Restrooms, locker rooms, health and physical education classes, competitive athletics, overnight field trips, homecoming courts and proms are just some of the explicitly gendered spaces that tend to be the most controversial because they require us to re-examine our beliefs about who belongs in those spaces. This can be challenging for everyone involved.

The following discussion seeks to bring people beyond those initial visceral reactions, provide tools to help guide others through that same process and lead to the creation of a school culture that values gender diversity and respect for all students.

Restrooms and locker rooms

Providing T/GE students with access to the restrooms and locker rooms that match their gender identity is yet another way that schools can adjust to meet students' individual needs (Seelman, 2014, 2016). Typically, the student, with or without their parents/caregivers, will approach an administrator to request that the school gives them access to the appropriate restroom and locker room. Generally, there is no reason to doubt the sincerity of a student who asserts a T/GE identity, and schools should accept the student's identity without imposing additional requirements. If a school administrator has credible doubts about a student's sincerity, however, they should note their concerns and request some documentation showing that the student has asserted a T/GE identity in other settings. Again, this scenario is very unlikely to occur and school officials should avoid assuming the role of gatekeeper. The experiences of schools that respect and affirm T/GE students by providing them with access to the restrooms and locker rooms that match their gender identity demonstrate that implementing such a policy is not only possible, but does not create the problems that some fear it will.

Restrooms and locker rooms can be a source of discomfort for everyone, not just T/GE students, and it is incumbent on school officials to ensure that all students are safe in the school's facilities. In schools that provide T/GE students with access to the facilities that accord with their gender identity, this has not been an issue. Access to gender-neutral bathrooms can address many of these concerns, and provide a safe and comfortable place for T/GE youth to use the restroom (Herman, 2013).

If other students have privacy concerns about using a restroom with a T/GE student, schools should attempt to address these and any other misconceptions that may be causing the students' discomfort. In those conversations, it is important to remind students that behaving in a way that makes others uncomfortable is unacceptable and a violation of the school's commitment to ensuring the safety of all students. It must also be clear that a T/GE student's mere presence does not constitute inappropriate behavior. Any student who feels uncomfortable sharing facilities with a T/GE student should be allowed to use another, more private facility, like the bathroom in the nurse's office, but a T/GE student should never be forced to use alternative facilities to make other students comfortable.

The key concepts—that respect for the T/GE student should be the starting point, that being uncomfortable is not the same as being unsafe and that school officials have a responsibility to ensure the safety of all students—can be applied to many situations that may arise when providing a T/GE student with access to the appropriate restroom and locker room.

Overnight field trips

Overnight field trips are important opportunities for social engagement for young people. Making sure that a T/GE student has access to all components of a field trip requires some planning for issues like room assignments, chaperones and showers. Schools have an obligation to set clear expectations about respecting one another's privacy and boundaries. As students share much closer quarters on field trips, explicitly naming expectations about what it means to be in a communal environment is critically important and will improve all students' experiences. A T/GE student's comfort level with sleeping arrangements will largely depend on the manner in which related issues are addressed. If students are to be separated based on gender, then the T/GE student should be allowed to room with peers that match their gender identity. As with any other students, the school should try to pair the T/GE student with peers with whom the student feels comfortable. Regardless of whether their roommates know about the student's gender identity, the school has an obligation to maintain the student's privacy and cannot disclose or require disclosure of the student's T/GE status to the other students or their parents.

If showering facilities are communal, the school should find out whether the venue has any single stalls or more private shower facilities that students can use. Recognizing that a number of students would likely prefer more privacy while showering, the school should consider creating a schedule to allow those students to use the shower facilities one at a time.

Competitive sports teams

Participating in sports teaches students many great skills and life lessons that will serve them well in the future. In order to ensure that T/GE students are able to engage in sports, several states have adopted eligibility rules that explicitly permit T/GE students to participate in school sports consistent with their gender identity. Conversely, there was a conservative movement in 2019–2020 in some states to restrict some of these rulings (Levin, 2020). Unfortunately, schools often erroneously believe that a T/GE student, particularly a T/GE girl, will have a competitive advantage over the other players and therefore should not be allowed to compete on the team that matches their gender identity. Concerns regarding competitive advantage are unfounded and often grounded in sex stereotypes about the differences and abilities of males versus females. Focusing on the perceived differences between males and females too often obscures the fact that there is great variation among cisgender males and among cisgender females. As such, while a T/GE girl may have been designated male at birth, she still falls within the wide range of athletic abilities of her female peers. Increasingly, T/GE youth are transitioning before puberty and, as part of their transition, are taking medication that prevents their body from going through their designated puberty, which means that—with the exception of their reproductive organs—T/GE students are just like their cisgender peers, including their hormone levels.

Health and physical education classes

For a variety of reasons, some schools maintain sex-separated health and physical education classes. Part of integrating a T/GE student into the school environment is to place them in the classes that match their gender identity. T/GE students frequently cite the lack of locker room access as a key factor in their inability to fully participate in physical education courses, which can create a barrier to meeting graduation requirements.

Homecoming, prom and other school traditions

School traditions are important to many students, and T/GE students are no exception. Schools should allow T/GE students to participate in all school traditions, including sex-separated traditions, in the gender category that matches their gender identity. For T/GE students who want to be seen by peers as their authentic selves, participating in traditions like running for homecoming king or queen or prom king or queen can be very affirming. Educators should look to the growing number of schools where students have elected their T/GE classmates to fill those roles for proof of the positive impact on the whole school community. Allowing T/GE students to participate in these traditions not only gives them validation from the school, but also from their peers.

Discrimination, harassment and bullying

It is the responsibility of each school and district to ensure that T/GE and gender-expansive students have a safe school environment, which includes ensuring that any incident of discrimination, harassment or violence is thoroughly investigated, appropriate corrective action is taken and students and staff have access to appropriate resources. Complaints alleging discrimination or harassment based on a person's actual or perceived T/GE status or gender expression should be handled in the same manner as any other discrimination or harassment complaints. While all school districts should have non-discrimination and harassment policies that cover gender identity, policies alone are not enough. Districts must also address bullying and harassment with research-based interventions. Research has shown that punitive policies requiring actions that remove students from their educational environments—such as "zero tolerance" policies that rely on suspension and expulsion—are detrimental to overall school climate (Russell, 2010). Instead of changing behavior, suspension and expulsion reinforce negative behavior and often harm the students these policies are meant to protect, because they are used disproportionately against LGBTQ students, students of color and students with disabilities. What this means in practice is that the LGBTQ student who fights back against bullying is more likely to be punished than the student who is the aggressor. Restorative justice programs and positive behavior interventions and supports are two examples of alternative discipline approaches that improve school climate and address the root cause of bullying and harassment. The most effective way to reduce bullying is to create a school-wide culture of inclusion and respect for difference.

School districts should adopt explicit non-discrimination and anti-bullying policies to help ensure acceptance, respect and safety for all students and compliance with all federal and state laws. The policy language included here regarding bullying, harassment and discrimination is not comprehensive, and districts are encouraged to consult GLSEN's *Local Education Agency Policy on Transgender and Nonbinary Students* for more comprehensive recommended policy language.[1]

Rights of T/GE youth

According to the National Center for Transgender Equality,[2] T/GE youth are entitled to the following rights as they pertain to school situations:

> Title IX is a federal law that makes sex discrimination illegal in most schools. Most courts who have looked at the issue have said that this includes discrimination against someone because they are transgender or because they don't meet gender-related stereotypes or expectations. Several other federal and state laws also protect transgender students. Here are some of the rights you have under these laws:
>
> - You have the right to be treated according to your affirmed gender identity.

---

1   www.glsen.org/activity/model-local-education-agency-policy-on-transgender-nonbinary-students

2   https://transequality.org/know-your-rights/schools, downloaded 04/27/2020

- You have the right to be called by the name and *personal gender* pronouns that match your affirmed gender identity.

- You have the right not to be bullied or harassed because you are T/GE or gender variant.

- You have the right to use restrooms and locker rooms that match your gender identity, and you can't be forced to use separate facilities.

- You have the right to get the same opportunities to learn and participate in school life as anyone else, no matter your gender, including your gender identity or expression, or your race, nationality, or disability.

- You have the right to dress and present yourself according to your affirmed gender identity.

- You have the right to protect your privacy and choose who you tell or don't tell about being transgender.

- You have the right to join or start an LGBT student club like a GSA or Pride Alliance. Your school isn't allowed to ban LGBT student groups or treat those groups differently than other students.

Legal issues

In addition to these rights, several laws protect T/GE students from discrimination at school:

- Title IX is a federal law banning sex discrimination in schools. Courts have made it clear that that includes discrimination against someone because they are T/GE or don't meet gender stereotypes or expectations. Title IX applies to all schools (including kindergarden to 12th grade schools and colleges) that get federal money, including nearly all public schools.

- State laws and school district policies in many places also protect T/GE students from discrimination. You can find information about some of these laws or policies at the National Center on T/GE Equality School Action Center's website.[3]

- Hundreds of school districts around the country also have policies that ban discrimination based on gender identity or expression.

- The Equal Access Act requires all student organizations, such as a Gay-Straight Alliance or Pride Alliance, to be treated equally. This means that schools cannot ban certain types of groups or single them out for worse treatment.

- The Family Educational Rights and Privacy Act (FERPA) protects personal information about students in school records, and in most cases, it makes it illegal for schools to share that information with others without permission from a student or (if the student is a minor) their parents/caregivers. This includes information about their T/GE status or medical history.

- The First Amendment of the US Constitution protects students' freedom of speech and freedom of expression. That includes the right to dress according to your gender identity, talk about being T/GE openly, and express your gender in other ways.

Recommendations for schools to create trans-affirming environments

There are many excellent examples of guidelines to support T/GE students, including sample policies and very specific guidelines. There is no need to reproduce these here, as those that exist online can be modified and tailored to fit the needs of the specific district or school system. There are two excellent examples:

- New York City Department of Education's Guidelines to Support Transgender and Gender Expansive Students.[4]

---

3   https://transequality.org/schoolaction
4   www.schools.nyc.gov/school-life/school-environment/guidelines-on-gender/
guidelines-to-support-transgender-and-gender-expansive-students

- GLSEN's Model School District Policy on Transgender and Gender Nonconforming Students.[5]

In addition, the following suggestions are offered for school districts taking steps to establish and maintain a non-discriminatory environment for all students, including T/GE and transitioning students.

- School districts should ensure that a T/GE student is addressed at school by the name and personal gender pronoun chosen by the student, regardless of whether a legal name change or change in official school records has occurred.

- School districts should issue school documentation for a T/GE student, such as student identification cards, in the name chosen by the student.

- T/GE students should be allowed to dress in accordance with the student's gender identity. Dress codes should not be enforced more strictly for T/GE and gender-diverse students than for other students.

- School districts should develop policies and procedures to ensure that their schools provide a safe and supportive learning environment that is free from discrimination and harassment for T/GE students, including students going through a gender transition.

- All school districts should review and update their existing policies and procedures, including those regarding classroom activities, school ceremonies, school photographs and dress codes, to verify that T/GE students are not excluded.

- School districts must comply with laws and regulations which prohibit harassment, intimidation and bullying, and require that each district board of education develop, adopt and implement a policy prohibiting harassment, intimidation or bullying on school property, at a school-sponsored function or on a school

5   www.glsen.org/activity/model-district-policy-transgender-and-gender-nonconforming-students

bus. If harassment based on gender identity creates a hostile environment, the school must take prompt and effective steps to end the harassment, prevent its recurrence and, as appropriate, remedy its effects.

- School districts should provide administration, faculty and all staff training on sensitivity and respect towards T/GE students.

- School districts should honor and recognize a student's affirmed gender identity, and should not require any documentation or evidence in any form, including diagnosis, treatment or legal name change.

- A school's obligation is to ensure non-discrimination on the basis of gender identity and requires schools to provide T/GE students with equal access to educational programs and activities, even in circumstances in which other students, parents/caregivers or community members raise objections or concerns.

- Since the classroom is the heart of the learning experience for students in educational systems, discussion about T/GE issues and a recognition of the contribution of T/GE people to history, literature, arts, science and modern society should be integrated into all subject areas and departments in an age-appropriate fashion.

- School personnel may not disclose information that may disclose a student's T/GE status except as allowed by law. Schools are advised to work with the student to create an appropriate confidentiality plan regarding the student's T/GE or transitioning status.

- With respect to gender-segregated classes or athletic activities, including intramural and interscholastic athletics, all students must be allowed to participate in a manner consistent with their gender identity.

- T/GE students must be provided with the same opportunities to participate in physical education as other students in accordance with their gender identity.

- T/GE students must be permitted to participate in gender-segregated school activities in accordance with their gender identity.

- The formation of student clubs or programs regarding issues related to lesbian, gay, bisexual, T/GE and queer/questioning (LGBTQ) youth must be permitted and supported.

- Support should be offered in the creation of peer-led educational groups.

- School districts should allow a T/GE student to use a restroom or locker room based on the student's gender identity or initiate the use of gender-neutral bathrooms (toilet facilities that anyone may use, irrespective of gender identity or gender expression).

WHAT CAN YOUTH WORKERS DO?

The following are recommendations for promoting competence with respect to working with T/GE students and their families:

- Break the silence that surrounds issues of gender identity expression and affirm all forms of diversity.

- Work toward making the environment a safe one for T/GE youth. Schools need to foster an environment where name-calling and slurs of all types are unacceptable. Schools must have a written policy for addressing physical violence of all types. Administrators should address physical violence swiftly, placing the blame clearly on those perpetrating the violence, not on the T/GE youth for being out about their identity.

- Schools must establish environments where it is safe for T/GE adults to be as open about their orientation as it is for non-T/GE staff. Role-modeling by T/GE adults will benefit all students, not just T/GE students.

- Schools must involve parents/caregivers as much as possible in discussions about gender, sexuality and sexual identity issues. Parental education is a key factor in abolishing myths and stereotypes, as well as an effective means for reducing the stigma associated with being T/GE.

- Schools should support LGBTQ+ alliances such as the Gay, Lesbian, Straight Educators Network programs or Project 10 programs, which can be found across the country.

The stressful experiences encountered by many T/GE youth in educational settings are cumulative and detrimental to educational performance, but also to self-esteem and sense of self-worth. Teachers, coaches, teachers' aides, clerical staff, maintenance and dietary staff, social workers, guidance counselors and administrators all play key roles in both mitigating and enhancing the negative effects of the stressors associated with school life for many T/GE youth. School boards must also set standards for addressing these issues.

Conclusion

All school administrators—superintendents, principals and others—have an obligation to ensure that a safe, respectful and supportive learning environment is provided for all students. This is especially important with regard to T/GE students and others whose gender expression differs from the norm, because a growing body of evidence indicates that these young people are often targets of harassment, discrimination, bullying and violence in school settings.

School administrators, especially the school principal, are responsible for fostering a school climate that supports the learning and healthy development of all students. Creating an inclusive, welcoming school environment for all students is the responsibility of the school's administration. This is done in part by having strong anti-bullying and anti-discrimination policies and ensuring that these are enforced. It is at least as important to take a more proactive stance by communicating regularly with all staff and students about how to build a positive school culture and how to create a shared school community where individual differences are accepted and celebrated and where all students feel included and respected, regardless of their gender expression. School administrators should ensure that all students' basic rights are upheld. They should be aware that the US Department of Education advises that T/GE and gender-variant students are covered by Title IX, the federal law that prohibits discrimination based on sex in schools, and they should be aware of resources that could assist them in developing school-wide policies that affirm all young people, including T/GE students.

One of the most important factors in ensuring a safe and supportive environment for T/GE students is communication between the school/district and student. In the spirit of a student-centered approach, school district personnel should have an open, but confidential, discussion with the student to ascertain the student's preference on matters such as chosen name, chosen personal gender pronoun, and parental communications.

T/GE students across the US and internationally continue to face hostile school climates that threaten their academic and psychological well-being, and it is increasingly important to turn attention to the ways that schools, educators and advocates can promote safer and more welcoming learning environments for T/GE youth.

CHAPTER 5

Discrimination and Anti-T/GE Harassment and Violence

While the visibility of T/GE people is increasing in popular culture and daily life, many continue to face severe discrimination, stigma, harassment and systemic inequality. T/GE youth face challenges within their families, at school, in foster care, in juvenile justice systems, in homeless systems and in the communities where they live and deal with the impact of oppression and stigma on a daily basis.

In this context, *stigma* is defined as a metaphorical blot on one's identity, and it is one factor that makes T/GE youth different from their cisgender counterparts (see Goffman's (1963) classic work on this topic). T/GE youth live with the knowledge that their identity as a T/GE person is stigmatized and despised by society (Bockting *et al.*, 2013). Although T/GE people have increasingly gained acceptance from mainstream culture, some people still view a T/GE identity as a stigmatizing status, something to hide or to be ashamed of, and this stigma causes young people a great deal of stress.

A stigmatized person is seen as different or as "other," thus devaluing, leading others to see that person as flawed or inferior. People who are seen as stigmatized face socially condoned exclusion, discrimination and violence. For T/GE youth, this means that they deal with stigma-based ignorance, stereotypes, prejudice, victimization and discrimination based on their gender identity and gender expression.

The cultural discrimination messages that are conveyed to T/GE youth and their families are embedded in the binary concepts of language that we hear every day:

"Is the baby a girl or a boy?"

"She is such a pretty girl."

"Boys will be boys."

Most of us grew up without an awareness of gender diversity and these aforementioned cultural messages are also incorporated into the institutional systems with which we interact. Dealing with a gender-ignorant worker at the Department of Motor Vehicles, or a school system that cannot seem to address a young person by the personal gender pronoun that they have asked them to use, adds extra layers of distress and hardship for a T/GE young person.

When a T/GE young person lives within multiple environments with gender-based minority stressors such as violence, family distress, bullying behaviors, harassment, family rejection, lack of gender affirmation, isolation and lack of overall respectful treatment, they are at risk of increased levels of psychological distress. Brill and Kenney (2016), Newcomb *et al.* (2020) and Rood *et al.* (2016) all suggest that the higher the level of minority stress, the higher the level of risk of problems such as substance abuse, anxiety, mood disorders, risky sexual behavior, self-harm and many other possible disorders.

External stressors (Burgess, 2009) that can have a negative impact on T/GE youth include:

- *Verbal and physical victimization*—T/GE youth are highly vulnerable to threats to their safety. These include bullying by peers or adults, harassment, harm to personal property, and physical and/or sexual violence.

- *Rejection*—gender-based rejection may be one of the most harmful forms of external stress. Rejections directly impact how a young person feels about themselves. Losing friends, feeling no longer welcome, or made to feel uncomfortable in their own home, and not being allowed to play sports on a team of their affirmed gender are all possible rejections that can cause harm and hurt to a T/GE young person.

- *Gender non-affirmation*—this is when a T/GE young person has to repeatedly explain their gender identity to others and repeatedly correct personal gender pronoun usage, has others invalidate their appearance or body and is frequently misgendered because others do not see gender as they do.

Internal stressors include:

- *Internalized transphobia*—when a young person believes the negative messages they are hearing about their gender, they can feel embarrassment, hatred, fear or shame about who they are.

- *Negative expectations for the future*—this is the constant avoidance of any upsetting or dangerous situations, almost expecting rejection or victimization from others. They are constantly scanning for safety in all environments. Such behavior drains energy, which might be used for more useful purposes.

- *Keeping stealth*—concealment of a T/GE young person's identity can leave a young person feeling isolated, alone, fearful and less likely to interact and engage with other T/GE people.

What does the data say?

The National Center for Transgender Equality's *Report of the 2015 U.S. Transgender Survey* (James *et al.*, 2016) collected and analyzed data from 27,715 adult respondents from all 50 US states. Findings revealed concerning patterns of mistreatment and discrimination and disparities between T/GE people in the survey and the US population with regard to the most basic elements of life, such as finding a job, having a place to live, accessing medical care, and enjoying the support of family and community. Although this survey did not include youth below the ages of 18 years old, many findings can be extrapolated from this data.

Respondents reported high levels of mistreatment, harassment and violence in every aspect of life. One in ten (10%) of those who were out to their immediate family reported that a family member was violent towards them because they were T/GE, and 8 percent were kicked out of their home because they identified as T/GE. The majority of respondents who were out or perceived as T/GE while in school (K–12) experienced some form of mistreatment, including being verbally harassed (54%), physically attacked (24%) and sexually assaulted (13%) because they were T/GE. Further, 17 percent experienced such severe mistreatment that they left a school as a result (James *et al.*, 2016).

Further findings provide a troubling portrait of the impact of stigma and discrimination which is built into the health care systems for many T/GE people. An astounding 39 percent of respondents experienced serious psychological distress in the month prior to completing the survey, compared with only 5 percent of the US population. Among the most concerning findings is that 40 percent of respondents had attempted suicide in their lifetime—nearly nine times the attempted suicide rate in the US population (4.6%). Respondents also encountered high levels of mistreatment when seeking health care. In the year prior to completing the survey, one third (33%) of those who saw a health care provider had at least one negative experience related to being T/GE, such as being verbally harassed or refused treatment because of their gender identity. Additionally, nearly one quarter (23%) of respondents reported that they did not seek the health care they needed in the year prior to completing the survey due to fear of being mistreated as a T/GE person, and 33 percent did not go to a health care provider when needed because they could not afford it.

With respect to survey respondents who had experienced harassment and violence:

- nearly half (46%) had been verbally harassed in the past year because of being T/GE

- nearly one in ten (9%) had been physically attacked in the past year because of being T/GE

- nearly half (47%) had been sexually assaulted at some point in their lifetime, and one in ten (10%) had been sexually assaulted in the past year.

This data is troubling for T/GE youth, who in many cases may be even more vulnerable than their adult counterparts who participated in this study. Given that there are chapters in this book focusing on school issues, health and mental health, this chapter will not focus on harassment, discrimination and violence that T/GE youth may face in those systems. It will, however, focus on issues pertaining to the lack of legal protections for T/GE young people; harassment and stigma; anti-T/GE discrimination; obtaining legal documents; discrimination towards T/GE people of color; and discrimination towards T/GE youth by the LGB community.

The lack of legal protection

In June of 2020, the US Supreme Court ruled that a landmark civil rights law *does protect* gay and T/GE from workplace discrimination, handing the movement for LGBT equality a long-sought and unexpected victory (Liptak, 2020).

This highlighted a number of issues critical to the LGBT community— bathrooms, locker rooms, sports, personal gender pronouns and religious objections to same-sex marriage. The decision, the first major case on T/GE rights, came amid widespread demonstrations, some protesting at violence aimed at T/GE people of color. Until this decision, it was legal in more than half of the US states to fire workers for being gay, bisexual or T/GE. The decision thus extended workplace protections to millions of people across the nation. The court's ruling suggested that a new era in T/GE rights had arrived.

According to the Human Rights Campaign's 2019 State Equality Index, the majority of states (44) and the District of Columbia prohibit discrimination based on sex in public accommodations. Many state courts and enforcement agencies have interpreted these laws to protect T/GE people.

Several states and localities also explicitly prohibit discrimination based on gender identity and sexual orientation in public accommodations. The following 17 states have explicit protections: California, Colorado, Connecticut, Delaware, Hawaii, Illinois, Iowa, Maine, Maryland, Minnesota, Nevada, New Jersey, New Mexico, Oregon, Rhode Island, Vermont and Washington State; as well as the District of Columbia. More than 200 cities and counties also explicitly prohibit gender identity discrimination even if their state does not.

Rights in public accommodations

According to the National Center for Transgender Equality,[1] most states and many cities prohibit discrimination in public accommodations based on either sex or gender identity. If a state or locality has such a law, individuals have the following rights:

- The right to not be refused entry, participation or services because one identifies as T/GE. Individuals have the right to enjoy a business's services or goods on an equal basis.

- The right to dress and present oneself in a manner consistent with one's affirmed gender identity. Individuals cannot be turned away because someone objects to their gender presentation.

- The right to be free from harassment. If the business's management knows of serious harassment by staff or customers and fails to remedy it, this may be discrimination.

Conversely, state legislatures across the country are debating—and in some cases passing—legislation specifically designed to prohibit T/GE youth from accessing public bathrooms that correspond with their gender identity. They are also attempting to stop physicians from prescribing hormones for T/GE youth, stop T/GE youth from playing on sports teams, and creating exemptions based on religious beliefs that would allow discrimination against LGBTQ people.

Verbal harassment

T/GE inequality is the unequal protection T/GE people receive in work, school and society in general. T/GE people regularly face transphobia harassment. Ultimately, one of the largest reasons that T/GE people face inequality is due to a lack of public understanding of T/GE issues.

T/GE people are still often met with ridicule from a society that does not understand them. T/GE people are vulnerable to lawmakers who attempt to leverage anti-T/GE discrimination to score political points with conservative constituents; to family, friends and co-workers who

---

1   https://transequality.org/know-your-rights/public-accommodations, downloaded 04/03/2020

reject T/GE people on learning about their T/GE identities; and to people who harass, bully and commit serious violence against T/GE people.

T/GE young people are also at high risk for harassment and bullying from their peers (Grossman *et al.*, 2006a; Grossman *et al.*, 2006b; Sausa, 2005). Although verbal harassment is prevalent, even when T/GE youth do not experience overt harassment, they often encounter unsupportive environments (schools, recreational centers and in their neighborhoods) where people refuse to use their affirmed name and personal gender pronouns or when they are belittled for "using the wrong bathroom." Such microaggressions (defined as everyday actions—verbal or non-verbal slights, snubs or insults), whether intentional or not, communicate hostile, derogatory and negative messages to targeted people based solely on their marginalized status (Sue, 2010). Emerson's narrative exemplifies this phenomenon:

> I had this teacher who, even though I had told her several times that I identified as Emerson and used he/him pronouns, insisted on calling me by what she said was "my legal name." It made me feel so bad. Every day I had to deal with her and her refusal to use my affirmed name, and to be honest, it just wore me out. When I came home from school I had to sleep for about two hours to recover.

These messages, hurled day after day at a T/GE young person, demean them, invalidate their reality as a T/GE person and communicate that they are "less than" a human being. While some might downplay the harmful nature of microaggressions, claiming that they are "small acts," they have a cumulative and deleterious effect on the mental health and well-being of T/GE youth (Sue, 2010).

According to research by Grossman and D'Augelli (2006, 2007), nearly three-quarters of T/GE youth experience verbal abuse from their own families. More than a quarter of them report that they had been slapped or beaten. Young T/GE women are at highest risk for physical abuse within their homes (Koken, Bimbi & Parsons, 2009) and there are correlations drawn from the work of Ryan and colleagues (2009, 2010) between physical and verbal abuse and suicide attempts. For many T/GE young people, the risky behaviors in which they may engage emerge as a coping strategy for dealing with the almost daily stress of managing harassment, discrimination and violence in various contexts (Haas, Rodgers & Herman 2017).

Anti-T/GE violence

The potential for violence is a reality for many T/GE youth. Dane recalls this experience:

> I lived in a shelter, and one night on my way home from being out with friends, these boys who lived in the shelter started saying shit to me—calling me a tranny and making disgusting comments. I just couldn't take it anymore and I made some shady comment back to them. I didn't expect it, but two of them just started punching me, and when I stumbled, they kicked me. I tried to defend myself, but with three of them and one of me, I couldn't. I finally got my footing and ran away. But my face was bruised and my knees were all cut up. When I entered the shelter, I was clearly upset and they noticed my injuries and asked what happened. I told them I got mugged; they asked if I wanted to call the police and I said no—what were they gonna do? They don't protect T/GE people—it would have been more humiliation on top of what I already felt.

T/GE people have few options for protecting themselves from violence or seeking justice. The National Center for Transgender Equality (NCTE) found that 22 percent of T/GE adults who had interacted with police experienced bias-based harassment from them, with T/GE people of color reporting much higher rates. Twenty percent reported having been denied equal service by law enforcement. Nearly half of the T/GE people surveyed in the study said that they were uncomfortable turning to police for help.

T/GE individuals are disproportionately affected by hate crimes, and some could argue the current justice and legal systems are not equipped to manage such crimes. However, T/GE individuals are less likely to report transphobic violence because of their distrust for law enforcement officials. According to the National Center for Transgender Equality, which collected data from T/GE adults, not youth, "One-fifth (22%) of respondents who have interacted with police reported harassment by police, with much higher rates reported by people of color" (Grant *et al.*, 2011, p.158). Overall, T/GE individuals face discrimination by government agencies. The National Center for Transgender Equality also reports, "One fifth (22%) were denied equal treatment by a government agency or official; 29 percent reported police harassment or disrespect; and 12 percent had been denied equal treatment or harassed by judges or court officials" (Grant *et al.*, 2011, p.158).

Identity documents

The widespread lack of accurate identity documents among T/GE people can have an impact on every area of their lives, including access to public services. Without identification, one cannot travel, register for school or access many services that are essential to function in society. Many states require evidence of medical transition—which can be prohibitively expensive and is not something that all T/GE people want—as well as fees for processing new identity documents, which may make them unaffordable for some members of the T/GE community. The National Center for Transgender Equality found that among adult respondents who had already transitioned, 33 percent had not been able to update any of their identity documents to match their affirmed gender. Tracy makes this observation about the lack of identity documents as it relates to discrimination:

> I couldn't even get a job at McDonald's. When I went into a place and tried to get a job, I did great with the application and the interview, but when I had to show my non-drivers' ID and my Social Security card, that's when it all fell apart. I presented as Tracy, but when my documents said my name was John, they wouldn't hire me. They just never called back—it was just so frustrating and upsetting.

T/GE people and unequal treatment in the LGBT community

Beginning in the 1990s, lesbian and gay activist organizations started to add T/GE people to their cause because at that time T/GE people faced many of the same prejudices. During this time, the gay and lesbian community frequently thought they were doing the right thing to bring T/GE people under their umbrella of defending the interests of and "serving the needs of all gay Americans" (Mallon, 2017, p.212). However, unintentionally, due to this description many associated the term T/GE with being gay.

Additionally, some members of the lesbian, gay and bisexual communities are uncomfortable with T/GE individuals and their issues, believing that T/GE issues and lived experiences are very different from their LGB experiences. In my own interviews with T/GE young people, they encountered tokenism while working in LGB organizations, claiming that "they include the 'T,' they need a T/GE representative as part of the organization, but they really don't do anything to truly support T/GE clients in their programs." T/GE young people in such situations recalled that they encountered being the only T/GE person responsible for knowing anything about being T/GE. When staff in the organizations had questions about T/GE issues they were always referred to the T/GE person who was expected to act as if they represented the views and experiences of every T/GE person. The LGB community's display of transphobia and heterosexism in some cases adds to the inequality that many T/GE people experience. One MSW field work student placed in an LGBT aging agency puts it well:

> I am an out trans person and they put me in this LGBT organization thinking I would be fine and they would accept me because they were a gay agency—but those bitches were just as mean and hostile to me as many straight people have been. It was very disappointing, but when you have experienced as much disappointment as I have, you kinda get used to it.

As the fight for equal rights for T/GE people moves forward, it has become apparent that the "T" in LGBT is being neglected and many gay, lesbian and bisexual people continue to take precedence (Currah, Juang & Minter, 2006; Green, 2017; Thaler, Bermudez & Sommer, 2009). By being part of the same-sex acronym, T/GE individuals are rarely recognized as a unique group that requires its own specific agenda to obtain equality. Instead, they are often considered an obscure and misunderstood subgroup of the gay community. Many individuals in the LBG community do not identify with T/GE people, and believe that gay rights and T/GE rights should be separated.

Discrimination against T/GE youth of color

Many believe that T/GE individuals of color face additional financial, social and interpersonal challenges as a result of structural racism in comparison to the T/GE community as a whole; however, others cite a lack of evidence for this belief (Glenn, 2009). According to the National Transgender Discrimination Survey, the combination of anti-T/GE bias with structural and individual racism means that T/GE people of color experience particularly high levels of discrimination. Specifically, black T/GE people reported the highest level of discrimination among all T/GE individuals of color. Studies about the T/GE community are extremely rare, and even fewer studies have been conducted on the experiences of T/GE individuals of color. However, some literature has documented the experiences of certain minority groups and the unique challenges they face in everyday life.

Often these studies are based on the theories of intersectionality and privilege. Intersectional approaches argue that the overlapping racial and gender identities of T/GE people of color results in them experiencing even more oppression and discrimination (Chan, 2018; Hatchel & Marx, 2018; Olivet & Dones, 2016). Therefore, T/GE advocacy should give special attention to non-white individuals. In this context, the theory of privilege asserts that both white T/GE individuals and cisgender people of color receive certain benefits because of their skin color or gender identity, while those who are both non-white and non-heterosexual are deprived of these benefits and face additional oppression (Hatchel & Marx, 2018; Singh, 2013).

Addressing the overlapping racial and gender discrimination facing T/GE individuals of color has raised a level of debate both among scholars and the public (Hatchel & Marx, 2018; Singh, 2013). One advocated approach is to work within the existing binary sex classification system and grant legal rights to T/GE individuals based on their self-defined gender identity. Similarly, scholars who study race disagree about whether embracing existing race classifications helps or harms minorities. Much of the disagreement lies in the question of how racial and gender identities are formed. The essentialism, or nature, view states that these identities are fixed and inherent from birth, while the social constructionism, or nurture, view sees them as flexible and dependent on one's environment.

To simply cluster all T/GE youth of color into a homogenous category is misleading. T/GE youth of color come from very diverse backgrounds (e.g. American Indian, African American, Latinx and Asian American) and, as a result, there is greater diversity within groups than there is between groups. Additionally, it must be recognized that there are a myriad of self and community-designated terms for gender identity expression (e.g. queer or two spirited). We also must acknowledge the fluidity of gender and sexual identities and constructs. As a result, youth workers use T/GE as a placeholder, a designated space for the insertion of culturally specific terms and understandings of sexual and gender identities (e.g. "two-spirit" in the case of American Indian communities or "ambiente" among Latinos or "same gender loving" among African Americans). Additionally, it is imperative that youth workers who use this section as a guide to practice with diverse communities properly assess terminology and associated cultural and spiritual meanings for the individuals and groups they are working with, and utilize culturally specific understandings to frame interventions and community building. It is also important that youth workers do not "use" the young person to guide their practice and call it empowerment. Youth workers should instead do their own homework in exploring this area and if possible utilize the personal narratives and experiences of T/GE adults of color who might act as a cultural guide in helping a worker to understand their varied experiences of T/GE people of color communities.

T/GE youth of color report feeling pressure to choose between their racial, ethnic and gender identities; these youth are less likely to be involved in T/GE social and cultural activities than their white counterparts (Cruz, 2014; Hatchel & Marx, 2018). Youth workers engaging with T/GE youth of color need to be aware of the multiple issues these young people face. Youth workers must be aware that T/GE youth of color may have different issues regarding coming out to families, may need to juggle multiple allegiances, and negotiate multiple identities in communities where they live and interact.

Anti-T/GE harassment and violence

T/GE young people, unlike their cisgender counterparts, are targeted for attack specifically because of their gender orientation and gender identity expression. North American culture—pervaded by a transphobic ideological system that denies, denigrates and stigmatizes T/GE people—simultaneously makes T/GE invisible and legitimizes hostility, discrimination and even violence against them. Safety has always been an issue for T/GE individuals. T/GE youth must assess issues of safety in their lives on a daily basis. When T/GE young people engage in behaviors allowed for cisgender young people (such as walking down a street holding hands or kissing), they make public what Western society has prescribed as private. They are accused of flaunting their sexuality and are thereby perceived as deserving of or even asking for retribution, harassment or assault.

WHAT CAN YOUTH WORKERS DO?

Professionals faced with these harsh realities might ask what can be done. This inquiry is the reminder that all youth work professionals have an ethical and moral responsibility to create and maintain safe environments for *every* young person in their care. The foundation of this safety is at the very core of all youth development practice.

- Open a dialogue with all youth, not just T/GE youth, about dealing with and accepting diversity. Have open discussions with all youth about diversity in sexual orientation and gender identity expression.

- Include content on T/GE experiences when discussing human sexuality with all youth.

- Develop an anti-slur policy that protects all racial, cultural, ethnic, religious or sexual orientation and gender identity expression groups.

- Have written policies to address all forms of violence.

- Post a list of rules and regulations that clearly state that all people regardless of race, religion, sexual/gender orientation, culture, gender identity expression and ability are respected and celebrated.

- Have discussions about gender-appropriate behaviors and mannerisms and why they do not indicate one's sexual orientation and/or gender identity orientation/expression.

- Make sure that your organization has dialogues about the negative effects that discrimination and violence have for all youth, including T/GE youth.

- Make sure that adults model appropriate accepting behaviors for youth.

- Ensure that staff are accountable in the supervision and evaluation processes for their demonstrated skills in creating a safe environment and for unconditional acceptance.

While advocates continue working to remedy these disparities, change cannot come too soon for T/GE people. Visibility—especially positive images of T/GE people in the media and society—continues to make a critical difference; but visibility is not enough and comes with real risks to our safety, especially for those of us who are part of other marginalized communities.

Conclusion

As professionals, we must be aware of the ways in which harassment and violence can be a factor in a T/GE youth's access to validation, support and treatment. We must be ready to advocate for our young people in the areas which have been causing them distress, disadvantage and harassment. These arenas could include family, school, service organization or access to health or mental health services. T/GE young people of color face much higher levels of discrimination than their white peers and require professionals who are more attuned and responsive to these aggressions.

CHAPTER 6

Creating Healthy and Affirming Social Environments

Some organizations and programs are intentional about serving T/GE youth. However, many youth-serving programs in the US and internationally—including educational, health care, youth development, sports, recreational and employment programs—ignore, overlook or reject the presence of T/GE youth among those they serve.

Unless youth-serving programs positively acknowledge their presence and actively affirm their rights and dignity, these young people may feel compelled to keep their gender identity expression a secret. Having to keep secret such an essential part of life puts these youth at risk of negative mental and physical health outcomes. It is the role of the youth worker to approach all work with youth from a firm belief that every young person is of great value, irrespective of race, ethnicity, biological sex, health status, socio-economic background, sexual orientation or gender identity expression. Indeed, valuing youth is an ethical imperative—to acknowledge and serve T/GE youth equally and positively, along with cisgender youth. T/GE youth need and deserve help to survive in the face of family rejection and school harassment, against heightened rates of HIV, sexually transmitted diseases, suicide, victimization and violence, and against racial, cultural and socio-economic prejudice. Even more, they should be able to thrive as valued members of their communities. Anyone who provides services to young people has an obligation to promote the health and well-being of all the youth in the program, including T/GE young people. At the same time, providing a safe and supportive space for T/GE youth will also provide a safe space in which all youth can thrive.

This chapter is intended to offer guidance for youth-serving professionals, especially direct service professionals in such fields as youth development, education, health care and social work. Unless these professionals work in a program that is exclusively directed toward T/GE youth, they may not realize that their program includes T/GE, non-binary youth, or that transphobia has negative consequences for all young people in the program.

Transphobia affects everyone. It has serious consequences for T/GE youth, including high rates of morbidity and mortality as a result of violence, prejudice and discrimination. Violence is frequently directed at T/GE youth in schools and communities, and many T/GE youth experience isolation with consequent depression, lowered self-esteem and feelings of hopelessness.

Safe space can be defined as a place where any young person can relax and be fully self-expressed, without fear of being made to feel uncomfortable, unwanted or unsafe on account of biological sex, sexual orientation, gender identity or gender expression, race, ethnicity, cultural background, age or physical and mental ability. It is a place where the rules safeguard each person's self-respect and strongly encourage everyone to respect others. Affirming the rights and dignity of T/GE youth will benefit all youth.

Therefore, the goal of this chapter is to enable staff of mainstream youth-serving organizations to think about creating a safe and welcoming environment for T/GE youth by directly addressing transphobia among staff and young people. To that end, this chapter guides youth-serving organizations and professionals in:

- assessing the organization's internal climate and the staff's personal attitudes regarding gender identity

- developing pro-social and proactive policies and procedures

- taking a stand for the rights and dignity of T/GE youth

- developing positive attitudes and behaviors among staff and youth regarding T/GE people.

How the transphobic climate hurts T/GE youth

Many people in the US, and internationally, may be unaware of how a transphobic climate affects T/GE people, especially T/GE youth. Despite horrifying incidents that sporadically make headlines nationwide— such as the brutal murders of T/GE young people like Brianna Hill, Nikki Kuhnhausen and Yahira Nesby and other incidents unfortunately too numerous to mention—many people accept, overlook or ignore the hatred and violence directed at T/GE people.

Creating safe spaces for T/GE youth

T/GE youth must confront issues of personal safety every day. They may frequently face violence, threats of violence or the possibility of violence. T/GE youth have worth; they have abilities, talents and strengths. They deserve to be treated with the same dignity and respect that others receive. They deserve safe spaces and respectful treatment in youth-serving agencies, organizations and programs (McGuire & Conover-Williams, 2010).

All youth deserve support and an environment in which they are free to learn and free to socialize with peers without fear of harassment or violence. Safe, supportive environments are essential for young people who are T/GE.

Although T/GE youth do not always require special services designed for them, they do require services that are responsive to their needs. T/GE and non-T/GE youth can and should be integrated into existing youth services, but there are circumstances when specific trans-affirming services should be created. Youth workers should stay up-to-date on current law and policies that do not allow discrimination.

Tips and strategies for creating inclusive programs

Whether or not you know of any T/GE youth in your program, it is essential to create a safe space for young people who are, believe that they might be or have friends or family members who are T/GE. The organization's responsibility is to all of the young people in the program. Even if some youth-serving professionals may feel uncomfortable about gender identity expression, they owe it to the young people they serve to educate themselves and to help connect youth to the organizations, role models and resources they need. Creating programs that are inclusive of and sensitive to T/GE youth is not difficult, but it does require conscientious attention. The following suggestions may help:

- Assess your own values and beliefs regarding gender identity. Taking stock will help you to address your own internal biases, recognize your personal limits, identify areas for personal growth and enable you to serve all youth, including T/GE youth, in an open, honest, respectful manner.

- Make it clear that transphobic sentiments and actions have no place in the program. Develop a written policy regarding discriminatory words and behavior directed at T/GE youth, just as you would towards any bias remarks. Post the policy in public areas and develop clear guidelines for disciplinary actions. It can be as simple as: *In this program, we do not tolerate negative comments, remarks, jokes or slurs towards anyone regardless of race, ethnicity, gender identity, sexuality, culture, religion, language or ability. We respect everyone in this program.* This can send a powerful message about what your program stands for.

- When training students or staff to lead or facilitate workshops, include opportunities to practice responding to unacceptable language and behavior. At the same time, work proactively to address stereotypes and misperceptions that may exist among the youth in your program.

- Consider posting a Safe Zone sticker or poster, such as one that says: *A person displaying this symbol will be understanding, supportive and trustworthy if gay, lesbian, bisexual, trans, gender expansive or questioning youth need help, advice or just someone with whom they can talk.*

- Use inclusive and gender-neutral language. Discuss "partners" or "someone special" instead of always assuming a youth's prospective date or partner is of the opposite sex. If you are doing role plays, use gender-neutral names, such as Jordan, Parker or Quinn. This will allow T/GE youth to personalize the context to their lives rather than reject the role-play scenario as being irrelevant.

- Schedule training sessions to debunk myths and stereotypes. Define the differences between sexual orientation, sexual behaviour and sex, gender, gender identity and gender expression. Include information about gender identity throughout a training session or program. This will help to dispel myths about T/GE people.

- Provide peer support. Young people benefit by developing their leadership, communication and other pro-social skills and by seeing role models with whom they can identify. Ensure that peer leaders include youth who identify as T/GE.

- Ask T/GE youth and adults to participate in panel discussions or as speakers to share some of their experiences. This will create a safe space and an opportunity for youth to talk openly about transphobia, racism, sexism, classism and other forms of oppression.

- Build youth–adult partnerships into the program. Make sure that youth leaders include some who identify as T/GE. A program is more effective and sustainable when youth are partners in the design, development, operations and evaluation of the program.

- Consider working with students to develop T/GE alliances in area schools, if such alliances do not already exist.

- Hire adults who are T/GE, and who reflect the racial/ethnic/cultural make-up of the community being served, to work in the program as full- or part-time staff or volunteers.

- Include local groups that serve T/GE people in referral and resource lists. Make sure your referral and resource lists are easily available to all young people on the program.

- Know when and where to seek help. Be aware of appropriate referral agencies for crisis intervention, mental and physical health services and so on. Be aware of your personal and organizational limits, and accept that your organization may not meet every need.

Tips and strategies for meeting the needs of T/GE youth

In recent years, many programs for youth have witnessed an increased presence of youth who self-identify as transgender, non-binary, gender non-conforming or gender expansive. T/GE youth are increasingly claiming their right to define and express themselves in new ways. These new ways include—but are not limited to—social transitioning norms such as name change and personal gender pronoun use, and medical transitioning norms such as hormone treatment and gender-affirming surgery.

Professionals who work with T/GE youth, in particular, increasingly observe the diverse ways in which these young people choose to identify, including making the choice not to identify within the binary of male or female. Youth-serving professionals, parents/caregivers, families, peers and community members can play key roles in supporting the healthy development of T/GE youth. Respecting T/GE youth means taking responsibility for providing them with a safe and supportive environment.

The following recommendations may assist you as you consider how to create more affirming environments for T/GE youth.

- Don't make assumptions! Do not assume that you know a youth's gender, or that a youth has gender identity issues. Exploring gender is a healthy expression of personal development. Self-identification or self-acknowledgement is a crucial first step in a youth's identity development and self-expression.

- Create a safe space for open discussion. Work towards creating an affirming environment that supports non-binary gender expression and offers a safe space for open discussion. Use inclusive, affirming, non-presumptuous, non-judgmental and gender-neutral language. Create organizational norms of behavior and language with youth.

- Be informed and don't be afraid to examine your own beliefs. Most adults are products of a society that holds to rigid gender roles, and we have been influenced by our cultural background. We're taught what is feminine and masculine, female and male, and we expect that these binary categories do not change.

Recognize your level of comfort with different types of gender expression and how this can affect your interactions with young people. Don't be afraid to ask questions.

- Seek to fully understand gender identity. Each person's gender identity is natural to that person. Gender identity and sexual orientation are a part of each individual and often develop uniquely. Across human experience, gender identity may be experienced as a continuum. That is, some people do not experience gender solely as female or male. It is important for youth-serving professionals to educate themselves on gender identity, sexual identity, adolescent development and sexual and social stereotypes. Moreover, sexuality and gender expression are only two of the aspects integral to a whole person. It is important to maintain a balanced perspective in addressing the multifaceted issues of young people's development.

- Respect confidentiality. When a young person shares personal information about gender identity, you have gained their trust. A breach of this confidence can have dire consequences for the young person. If it truly becomes necessary to share the information, first get the young person's permission.

- Know when and where to seek help. Be aware of appropriate referral agencies for crisis intervention, mental and physical health services, emergency assistance, shelters and so on. T/GE youth can often be subject to abuse, homelessness, suicide, harassment and physical violence. Be aware of your personal and organizational limits and accept that your organization may not always be the best one to assist a young person in every area.

- Provide training for staff, board members, volunteers and youth. Up-to-date training is necessary to help staff develop sensitivity and skills to interact with youth and to prevent anyone from being derogatory to T/GE people. Be sure to provide T/GE youth with information that can help ensure their physical safety.

- Protect T/GE youth from harassment! Immediately protect T/GE youth from harassment in any form, whether perpetrated by other young people, staff or others. Make it clear that harassing and abusive behavior towards anyone will not be tolerated.

- Provide gender-neutral restrooms, if possible. Every person has the right to use the bathroom, irrespective of gender identity.

Tips and strategies for addressing the challenges that face T/GE youth

T/GE youth face several unique problems caused by the highly gendered societies in which they live. Overall, society in the United States relies on rigorously maintained concepts of gender and gender expression. This creates specific challenges for T/GE youth.

Challenges

- Deliberately incorrect and disrespectful use of names and personal gender pronouns—when a T/GE youth identifies as a particular gender (irrespective of biological sex), it is respectful to the youth's human dignity to use the name chosen and the pronouns appropriate to that particular gender. To persevere intentionally in the use of a prior name (a dead name) and other personal gender pronouns is to be deliberately disrespectful. T/GE youth can understand and sympathize with some confusion, so long as there is continuous progress and good faith in using the proper name and personal gender pronouns.

- Lack of access to appropriate restroom facilities—T/GE youth often lack safe access to public restrooms. They may be assaulted if they use the restroom that conforms to their gender identity, or forced to use a restroom that does not conform to their gender identity.

- Lack of access to appropriate locker room facilities—T/GE young people often have no safe access to locker room facilities that conform to their gender identity.

- Rigid dress codes that differ for males and females—wherever dress codes are enforced, they may create problems for T/GE youth.

- Confidentiality—T/GE youth may have unsupportive families and may even face violence and ejection from their home if their gender identity or gender expression is disclosed to the family.

- Lack of role models, lack of accurate information—T/GE youth often feel alone in the world. Few programs for youth employ T/GE people; few libraries offer information about biological sex and gender, gender identity or being trans.

Solutions to the challenges

- Names and/or personal gender pronouns—use the name and/or personal gender pronouns appropriate to the young person's chosen gender identity. Remember that it is essential to everyone's dignity to be called by their chosen name, and it is everyone's right to be recognized as the person they see themselves to be. Apologize if you use the wrong personal gender pronoun or the wrong name and move on without making too much of a big deal about it.

- Access to restroom and locker room facilities—educate staff and youth about gender identity expression. Make sure that everyone understands that T/GE youth want to use the restrooms and locker rooms that conform to their gender identity; they have no interest in spying on others using those places. If possible, designate gender-neutral restrooms and locker rooms.

- Dress code—make sure that the dress code, if any, in your program respects young people's rights to dress in a manner that conforms to their affirmed gender identity.

- Confidentiality—make sure that the program maintains confidentiality with regard to the gender identity, gender expression, sexual orientation and sexual behavior of all the youth in the program.

- Role models and accurate information—make sure that everyone in the program is aware that there is great human diversity regarding gender, including male and female certainly, but also going beyond these two genders. Search out T/GE support groups and trans-affirming, youth-serving organizations in your area and, if there are none, start one. Make sure that these groups and organizations are included on your resource lists and that your resource lists are available to all the young people in the program.

Ways transphobia affects everyone

Transphobia affects everyone and has serious consequences for all youth. It can:

- make many T/GE youth feel isolated, lonely and ashamed

- create an environment in which T/GE youth have to face harassment and even violence in their schools, communities and homes

- make some T/GE youth "act straight" to hide their gender identity

- force many T/GE youth to become sexually active before they really want to just so they can hide their gender identity

- contribute to the self-doubt that makes many T/GE youth turn to drugs or alcohol to numb their feelings

- cause many T/GE youth to drop out of school and/or run away

- cause many T/GE youth to think about and/or even attempt suicide

- allow cisgender people to act unkindly or even cruelly towards T/GE people and encourage bullying and cruelty toward anyone whose appearance or behavior isn't sufficiently "macho" or "feminine"

- force cisgender people to act more "straight," limiting their individuality and self-expression. Cisgender youth often choose their clothes, hair color/style, friends and even behavior to "prove" that they are not T/GE

- destroy family relationships. Some parents/caregivers, sisters, brothers and even grandparents break off their relationships with T/GE family members

- lead many cisgender youth to become sexually active before they really want to just to "prove" they are straight

- make it very hard for cisgender people and T/GE young people to be friends

- make it nearly impossible for people to appreciate diversity and the wonderful variety that exists among all people.

Determining safety

Because they are required from early ages to scan their environment for safety cues, T/GE youth become experts at determining whether their immediate environment is a safe one. They have to because so much depends on it. T/GE people learn to scan their environment to determine whether it is a safe environment for them to be open about their gender identity expression. T/GE youth are by definition outsiders, outside the norm, different. No matter how integrated a T/GE youth is into family, community or school, they may feel as though they still are not part of the majority. T/GE youth are frequently fearful of being judged or discriminated against because they are T/GE.

Historically, T/GE youth have had to struggle to find their community. As they are beginning to explore their identity, many believe that they are the only people who feel as they do. Living in such a state of isolation can cause a young person to become depressed, anxious and sad. At the same time, body issues can be a major concern for the young T/GE person. At some point when the T/GE youth begin to realize that they are not the only T/GE person in the world, they have a strong desire to find others "like them," as Tracy reports:

When I was first coming to terms with my identity, there was a lot of confusion and isolation. At times I thought I was the only T/GE kid in the world. In fact, at first, I thought I was gay, and then a bit later, when I read some information online about non-binary people, I realized my feelings were more akin to what people felt. I connected with other non-binary young people in a youth group I joined in a city near my town, and that made me feel so much better about myself.

Since some T/GE youth may have limited information about their own emerging gender identity, many embark on a quest to find "their kind." Until the last decade, many T/GE adults found their community in the bar scene. Given the presence of alcohol and the fact that bars are adult environments, these are not appropriate settings for young people to meet others. However, T/GE youth—like all youth—will sometimes find their way into bars. Thus, for many T/GE youth, these settings are the first introduction to the wider T/GE world. T/GE youth—again, like other young people—need to be able to socialize and meet peers in safe, healthy, non-erotic, alcohol-free settings.

The internet has become all pervasive in the lives of most people, including youth. Most T/GE youth in the 21st century may, at least initially, meet one another online. The internet has enabled T/GE youth to gain access to information and to one another in ways that were inconceivable before its inception. T/GE youth may use the internet for dating apps, for information and knowledge development and to identify services. While the internet is a huge source of information, its use by youth is not without risks. Negative aspects of internet use include online harassment and cyberbullying, scams and sexual solicitation. Youth workers should be aware of youth who might be more susceptible to these risks and be available to help them address these issues should they arise.

What services do T/GE youth need?

Basically, these young people need the same types of youth services that all youth need:

- Community-based youth centers that affirm all youth, regardless of gender identity.

- Drop-in centers where all youth can safely hang out.

- Youth discussion groups—or more creative alternatives, like art, rap or poetry groups.

- After-school programs for tutoring and studying.

- Recreational programs.

- Safe shelter programs if housing is an issue.

- School-based extracurricular sports, music and art activities.

- Service-oriented programs and volunteer opportunities.

- Educational or instructional groups.

- Life skills groups.

- Counseling services.

There has been a great deal of debate about the need to include T/GE young people in existing mainstream youth services programs rather than developing an array of specialized youth services for T/GE youth or, for that matter, for gay, lesbian and bisexual youth. Opponents of special services note that T/GE young people need to interact within the larger cisgender context of society, and claim that such programming promotes segregation rather than integration and "ghettoizes" T/GE youth. Those who favor programs geared specifically for T/GE youth claim that T/GE youth will not use generic services or services that are specifically lesbian, gay or bi related because they perceive them to be anti-T/GE or not attentive to their unique needs as young people. They also assert that special services could hire openly T/GE staff that could empathize with the struggles of T/GE youth and act as role models for their clients. Proponents of specialized services note that youth services practitioners are often uncomfortable, unskilled and untrained in working with T/GE youth, and moreover, many youth services settings may be generally unsafe places for a self-identified or even a perceived T/GE young person.

The solution lies in a combination of both types of youth services. Services designed especially with an understanding of T/GE youth development could provide programming with sensitivity to the issues important to the specific needs of T/GE youth, in an atmosphere where they feel safe (see Mallon, 2009). Ideally, special services could funnel T/GE youth to affirming agencies when required. For example, T/GE youth requiring life skills training could participate in these types of programs with non-T/GE youth. At the same time, however, generic services need to be able to respond to and create trans-affirming environments for these young people. In the final analysis, specialized services for T/GE youth would not be necessary if mainstream youth services agencies were held accountable for providing quality care to all children, including T/GE children.

Although it is preferable for all youth to be integrated into appropriate services, until youth services practitioners and their agencies become more knowledgeable and skilled in working with T/GE-oriented adolescents via training and technical assistance, it is recommended that specialized youth services programs be developed and funded to provide an array of options and serve as safe places for this underserved population of young people. Special environments for T/GE youth should be created when existing environments do not provide for their safety and well-being. In some settings, T/GE youth are given clear messages that they are not welcome.

Dane, a Latinx T/GE youth from New York, recounts this story:

> When I went to my local community center, all they did was play basketball, and I'm sorry, but I hate basketball. I tried to get involved with some of the youth activities, but I just didn't feel comfortable with all of those guys. I always felt like they were looking at me and judging me. I heard about this trans youth group at the Center in New York and it was very scary to go there by myself, but one night I went to a meeting. As soon as I walked in I thought, "Oh, thank God, there are other kids like me!" Finally, I could have some friends. Finding the youth group was the best thing that ever happened to me. I have friends, we hang out, sometimes we go to the Center, sometimes we just do what other kids do—go to the mall, go to the movies, you know, just teenager stuff.

Although it should be a goal for all youth service systems to provide affirming, safe environments for all youth, providers must also understand that T/GE-specific youth services mean that T/GE youth no longer feel like outsiders. They are places for them to be themselves. The stress of managing one's identity can be very tiring for a young person. Being able to let loose is very important. In such environments, young people can be themselves, which includes being physically affectionate in a way that cisgender youth take for granted. Because T/GE youth experience some level of stigmatization or safety-related issues, they are sometimes either unwelcome in existing youth services environments, or feel that they are unwelcome because they do not find a niche in such a surrounding.

Systemic responses: the need for alternatives and strategies

In order to create consistently safe environments, there must be system-wide policies and practices in place to support the individual responses described above.

First, providing information alone is not sufficient. There must be system-wide recognition of the fact that negative attitudes and discrimination against T/GE youth contribute significantly to the difficulties that these youth encounter. Youth care professionals need to acknowledge the existence of T/GE young people and develop ways to educate themselves—as well as the families of children in care—in order to understand the significance of sexual orientation and gender identity expression in young people's lives.

Supporting T/GE youth and their families requires service providers trained in family systems and competent to address gender identity expression issues in a sensitive way with young people and families. Part of the youth service provider's role is to work towards increasing the parents/caregivers' knowledge about T/GE adolescents, and to model and encourage non-judgmental and accepting attitudes and behavior towards young people.

Providing trans-affirming youth services can cause problematic public relations concerns, particularly if the system does not have a clearly defined policy to provide appropriate services for T/GE youth. Youth services administrators would be wise to think about how they can develop their programs or adapt existing services to ensure the safety of all program participants.

Another strategy for creating a safe environment can be found in transforming the youth services system into one which is proactively responsive to the needs of T/GE youth. Hiring openly T/GE staff in community-based and residential programs is one step in this process. T/GE youth interviewed in several studies identified openly T/GE staff as instrumental in making them aware that the environment was safe. Closeted staff sent a clear message: "It's not safe for me to be out here— so it's not safe for you to be out, either." Petra makes this comment:

> When I walked into the agency, I saw this woman who worked there who I recognized from a dance I went to in the trans community. She looked really panicked when she saw me and then very much avoided me. In fact, she went out of her way to stay away from me while I was there. When I was leaving the program she was also walking out and said to me, "Please don't tell anyone, okay? I can't be out of my job." I couldn't believe it. I never went back there again. I mean if the staff couldn't be open and didn't feel safe, then I knew I certainly couldn't.

Systematic and ongoing staff training and professional development for all levels of youth services personnel are also essential. Quinn, a non-binary youth, makes this comment about staff training:

> I don't know what they teach these workers in social work school or wherever they go, but they sure don't know anything about non-binary people. I think they should all be required before graduating to take a course—you know, a class to give them the language and to tell them about us. I am sometimes so shocked by how little staff really know about us; many of them still believe all of those old-time myths and stereotypes. It's amazing to me.

Existing youth services programs need to be particularly aware of two particularly underserved groups, as there are currently very few programs that focus on meeting their needs: T/GE youth between the ages of 12 and 15, and seriously emotionally impaired or developmentally challenged T/GE youths between the ages of 12 and 20. I am not suggesting that specialized programs be developed by youth serving agencies to meet these needs, but rather that these youth are vulnerable populations within an already at-risk population group, and they may require additional attention from youth workers.

WHAT CAN YOUTH WORKERS DO?

How can youth services agencies create environments that suggest safety and acceptance? On the basis of my own experiences in the field, I have developed ten recommendations for developing a safe agency environment that affirms the identity of every young person:

1. *Acknowledge that T/GE are among your clients.* Do not assume that all your clients are cisgender or even gay, lesbian or bisexual. Many times, workers make assumptions based on inaccurate information or misperceptions. Just as clients will tell you who they are when—and if—they feel ready, T/GE clients will come out if and when they feel that there is a safe environment in which they can disclose this information. Even if you do not think that you have T/GE youth in your organization, you probably do.

2. *Educate yourself and your co-workers about T/GE youth.* Familiarize yourself with the literature, bring in speakers or ask an openly T/GE professional to act as your "cultural guide" to teach you and others in your agency about T/GE issues.

3. *Use gender-neutral language.* If a practitioner uses language that assumes a person is cisgender (i.e. inquiring about a girl's boyfriend or husband), T/GE clients may not feel that the professional is knowledgeable about their orientation and may not share valuable information. The use of words and terms such as "partner" or "someone special in your life" are appropriate and it is important to use them.

4. *Use the words* trans, non-binary, transgender *and* gender expansive *in an appropriate context when talking with clients about diversity.* As youth workers, we try to be inclusive by specifically referring to the diverse groups of people that we encounter—Latino, African American, Asian American, developmentally challenged. Being inclusive means also mentioning and acknowledging the existence of T/GE people.

5. *Have visible signs in the waiting room or in your office that speak to the fact that it is a trans-affirmative environment.* Magazines, pamphlets or posters which have the words *gender, trans, transgender and gender expansive* printed on them let clients know that your sensitized agency is a safe place for them. If you put them up and they get torn down—and they might—put them up again and have a discussion about why they have such a strong impact on some people.

6. *Be prepared to change the culture of your organization.* Condemning all slurs about all people lets colleagues know that you do not think a joke is funny if it is at the expense of any group. This sends an unambiguous message that oppression hurts everyone. Chapter 10 suggests a framework for organizational transformation.

7. *If a client discloses to you that he or she or they are T/GE, acknowledge it and talk about it.* Don't just move on to other subjects. Talk about what it means to this client to be T/GE. Process the feelings with them. It's okay to let clients know that you may not be able to answer all of their questions, or even to acknowledge that you don't have a lot of information about what it's like to be a T/GE person. But it is critical that you are unconditionally accepting of the person, supportive of their struggle to come to terms with these complex issues, and willing to listen. It is also critical to then *do your own homework* and learn as much as you can about the experiences of T/GE young people.

8. *Do not confuse T/GE identity with lesbian, gay or bisexual identity.* There are differences between sexual orientation and gender identity expression. T/GE youth may identify as heterosexual, lesbian, bisexual, gay, asexual or pansexual. Knowing the aspects of each identity can be very useful.

9. *Research resources in the T/GE community.* Identify and become familiar with the resources that exist for T/GE young people in your area. If there are services in your area, visit them, get to know their staff. Be prepared to escort clients who might be scared to go to a trans-affirming agency for the first time.

10. *If you are T/GE identified yourself, consider coming out!* Visibility is powerful. But you do not have to be a T/GE professional to work with T/GE youth. It is of course important to have role models that reflect the diversity of the youth, but non-T/GE allies are also very important.

Conclusion

This chapter provided an overview of how the transphobic and gender-rigid climate in the US affects T/GE youth and the systems that serve them. Practical tips and strategies for assessing the environment in an agency can be useful in creating safe spaces and moving agencies towards being more T/GE affirming. In addition, examining plans intended to sensitize program youth, staff and volunteers to transphobic sentiments and actions is critical for developing these environments of safety. All young people deserve safe spaces to be themselves with their peers; T/GE youth deserve nothing less. The next chapter discusses the importance of developing relationships and dating in the lives of T/GE youth.

CHAPTER 7

Relationships and Dating

T/GE youth, like their lesbian, gay, bi and cisgender counterparts, enjoy developing relationships with peers—which includes dating and the development of romantic attachments. It is as natural for T/GE youth to date and to develop romantic attachments as it is for any youth to do this. In fact, if T/GE youth are permitted to develop developmentally and age-appropriate relationships during adolescence, it is less likely that they will have a biphasic adolescence later in their lives and it is more likely that they will develop fully as adults who envision having a healthy relationship in their lives (Blair & Hoskin, 2018; Iantaffi & Bockting, 2011).

T/GE youth, like all youth, want to be able to be involved in relationships. Like all youth, T/GE youth develop crushes, think a lot about other young people that they like, and spend a great deal of time looking at themselves to see how they compare with others. Dating is a natural part of all adolescence. Not being able to date someone you like because of the stigma that is associated with gender identity expression can be crushing for a T/GE youth.

Some may assume that T/GE young people are only involved with and interested in dating other T/GE people, but this is not the reality for all T/GE young people. Some do indeed date people on the T/GE spectrum, others date on the LGB spectrum and still others date cisgender young people. Quinn makes this observation about his dating history:

> I have dated cis men and cis women, I have dated guys who were gay and bi. For me, it's more about the person than how they identify. For me, it is about connection, honesty and just feeling an attraction on multiple levels.

Dating in the 21st century is complicated and challenging. Almost everyone—T/GE, lesbian, gay, bisexual or cisgender—fears rejection, at least on some level, as Tracy notes:

> Dating is hard enough when you are cis—it's like 18,000,000 harder when you are trans. And I am not trying to get all the pity and stuff, but it's true, it is harder. I believe, though, that I will find that person who is accepting of me—I just have to wait it out. You will probably find a lot of assholes before that, but it will happen.

Although online dating sites are often a way that relationships begin in the 21st century, they can be a poor substitute for actual face-to-face interaction. The internet has made it possible for T/GE youth who have access to computers to socialize and meet other T/GE youth online. This phenomenon has provided unprecedented opportunities for social interaction with others in the T/GE community.

Unfortunately, the apps aren't the most welcoming place for T/GE men and women. Mainstream apps like *Tinder*, *Grindr* and *OkCupid* have been slow to recognize the needs of their T/GE users. It wasn't until 2016 that Tinder made it possible for users to specify gender identities like "T/GE," "T/GE man," "T/GE woman" and "gender queer." A major issue is whether to disclose one's T/GE identity in a dating app bio. Listing it could potentially lead to a T/GE person's profile being suspended due to negative reports being made regarding their profile, them being abused, or even outed in real life. However, if they don't list their T/GE identity, it could lead to accusations of "misleading" those they match with, which could lead to extremely dangerous situations, as Finley notes here:

> Coming out as trans can be a really hard thing to do. I usually do it online, but I don't just say, "I am trans, take it or leave it." I usually say, "I am a trans person—male to female—and that's just who I am. It doesn't make me any less of a person, or any less of a good girl, and if you don't accept that—that is completely okay with me, but if you do accept it—that's really awesome and I would really like to keep talking to you."

If you are T/GE, there are lots of different ways to come out to those you date. And how each T/GE person decides to do it is a personal choice. If you're online dating, you can choose to come out before you ever meet the person in real life or come out right in your dating profile as Finley did. You can come out on the first date or wait for the second or third date. Many T/GE young people may want to make sure they have a connection with the person, because if they are not going to continue seeing them, then they don't need to be anxious about how they'll react. The difficult part is that there really is no natural way to slip it into a conversation.

There are bright spots, though: the creators of *@personals*, an Instagram account for lesbian, queer, T/GE and non-binary people looking for love via an old-school classifieds approach, are currently crowdfunding in the hopes of building an app. And in September 2019, *OkCupid* became the first mainstream dating app to add a dedicated space on profiles for the LGBTQ+ community to state their personal gender pronouns.

Meeting other T/GE young people can, depending on geography and the need to hide, be a difficult prospect for some T/GE youth. In large urban areas, T/GE youth groups and T/GE student alliances in schools make it possible for youth to get together, but in some localities, especially in suburban or rural areas, these opportunities may not exist.

T/GE youth frequently date people from a range of genders, at least initially. Quinn makes this comment:

> I identify as a non-binary guy. So, first, I dated girls because that was what I thought I was supposed to do. I had a lot of friends that were girls anyway, so I went out with a few on dates—but there wasn't anything there. They were nice and all that, but there was no chemistry. Then, after a while, when I got the courage, I went out with a few guys and it was much better. There was something special there. But then I would date girls again; just to be sure that it was better with guys. It was kind of back and forth for a while. Now, I just date who I am attracted to and I don't worry about whether they are male or female.

For some T/GE young people, the dating challenges require a range of strategies, as Lee notes in this narrative:

I met this gal who I liked. We had two dates, and on the second date I decided I should tell her about myself. I started by telling her, "There is something I should probably tell you about myself." She looked like I was about to tell her that I was a vampire or something.

"I'm trans, I was designated female at birth, though I identify as a man. I wanted to tell you now because I'd like to continue to get to know you, but don't want to waste either of our time if this is a deal breaker for you."

She looked at me without saying anything. Which provided enough time for me to think of the worst scenarios. Then she broke her silence, and said: "Thank you for sharing that with me. Your honesty is impressive and an attractive quality. But that's a lot to take in. Not bad mind you, just a lot because it's different from what I've imagined or been able to see for myself. I might need to sit with it for a bit."

She did sit with it and I appreciated that, and she concluded that it was too big a stretch for her and was as polite as someone can be when she told me. It still hurt, but I respected her thoughtfulness.

For some T/GE youth, the potential of harassment and violence is an issue, as Ariel notes in this recollection:

Rejection for a trans person can be accompanied by violence— verbal assault or physical assault. Dating as a trans person can be life threatening. And even when it's not, it can still be scary. I have also had some experiences that were very transphobia. I had this one guy who went to my high school and he was very transphobic to me and clocking [watching] me, and that was not fun and I was not safe. Afterwards, I went and sat with my mom and cried. Dealing with him was really not safe and it was really scary.

Another subject that can quickly get awkward to navigate is when dates want to ask questions about growing up, as Carter recalls:

I went on a date with a woman I had met online—the site said we were an 85 percent match, so I was hopeful that she was progressive and gonna be cool with me. Halfway through dinner she asked me if

I had played sports in high school and without thinking I said, "No, I mean I tried out for the basketball team but I got cut." She looked at me confused: "Aren't you a little short to play basketball?" I had forgotten that she wouldn't have known that in high school I would have actually been trying out for the women's team. And while yes, I'm still short to play women's basketball, it wasn't as much of a reach. I smiled awkwardly and replied, "Probably why I got cut." She nodded, signaling to me that my story checked out. It was a stressful date.

Many T/GE youth have had positive experiences with dating, as Emerson notes:

From the perspective of a trans man, you meet people the same way other people meet—there are dating apps, LGBT apps and the old-fashioned just getting out and meeting people; doing hobbies, finding someone with similar interests by just going out and finding people like you—I think that is universally true whether you are trans or not.

But actually, engaging and dating, that's when things get a little more complicated for trans people. I try to follow three things for dating: be open, be honest, be genuine. I think this is important for any person dating, but specially for trans people. You don't want to feel like you are hiding anything—you don't want anyone to think you have anything to hide. You definitely need to come out to whomever you are dating as soon as possible, but that is a little more complicated for trans people. Dating is all about getting to know the other person, and if being trans is a major part of your life, you want them to know that—you don't want to pretend that you are something you're not. I think, as a trans person, you have gone against all odds to be yourself and that is important for someone to know. So, when it is time to tell the person you are dating that you are trans, it can be a little scary. I have this tip: test the waters by incorporating the subject into the conversation.

Trans topics are really big right now, so it is not that difficult to work it into a conversation. There are a lot of ways to bring that up and to see how they react—so that way you have a general idea and you know where you can go from there. Obviously, if they are super hateful and transphobic that will make things awkward, but you shouldn't feel regretful about bringing up the topic, because eventually it would come up, and if they have an issue with it, then that is someone you wouldn't want to be with anyway.

I think if you just portray being trans as another interesting part of who you are, then that is how they are gonna see it. If you make it this huge confession, guilt issue, then that's how they will see you and it will definitely be a big red flag for them. I know that is hard for some people, but there is nothing wrong with being transgender—it does not make you any less desirable as a partner and you have to go into this, knowing that. I know dating can be scary, but as long as you stay true to yourself, you will find that special someone.

Ariel, another T/GE young person, discusses the issue of boundaries to consider when dating:

I think it is so important to discuss boundaries. Discuss what you are comfortable talking about and what you are not. Discuss how comfortable you are talking about your body, and what makes you uncomfortable.

Carter makes these observations about dating:

I have to find a woman who can accept me. I have to find a woman who can be okay with the fact that my anatomy cannot give her children like a cis man. I have to find a woman who is okay with my genitals, who is okay with my scars.

It sounds scary, it may even sound like it is impossible, but there are people out there who are okay with me.

One of the first things for me is to be completely transparent with the women that I engage with romantically. I can never understand why someone would wait to tell their partner about being trans until the moment before they become intimate—to each their own, but I would never put myself or my partner in that position. Being trans, many of us have our guards up and we have issues with things like even taking our clothes off in front of another person—so you need boundaries, but you also have to be willing to talk it out.

Finley notes how family and friends' reactions may also need to be considered:

> The other issue is what are her friends gonna think, what is her family gonna think—do I even want them to know? The reality for me is that people are gonna judge. Trans people may be more accepted, because we are more visible, but you and your partner are gonna have to accept the fact that not everybody is gonna accept you. Not everyone is gonna be respectful of your relationship. Keep an open mind and be open to discussing the relationship with the people you care about. Remember why you are invested in your partner, what you like about them, and how they make you happy.

Feeling that it may be easier to find acceptance, some T/GE youth date other T/GE people, but some T/GE people identify as gay, others as lesbian, some as heterosexual, and still others in a non-binary way as trans. Quinn makes this observation:

> Pretty much everyone I have dated has identified as being somewhere in the LGBTQ community in some way. I feel that they better understand that my relationship to gender is not gonna be the same as a cisgender person's and that's cool, that's fine. People sometimes think we are fundamentally different from other people and we're not, we're just people. Some people are gonna be far outside the binary, and some people are gonna identify closer to the way cisgender people identify. It's one facet of who we are. In the end, people who are gonna love you, are gonna love you.

Youth who have opportunities to date people they are attracted to emerge as healthier adolescents. Dating for adolescents is a normal part of adolescent development.

Avoiding double standards

If the organization that you work for has policies about youth who participate in your programs and who are dating, it would be a good idea to make sure that these policies are gender neutral and that all young people are aware of them. It is also a good idea to either ignore them or enforce them evenly for both opposite-gender relationships and same-gender relationships.

In many cases, what is inappropriate behavior for opposite-gender couples is also inappropriate behavior for any couples who are dating. Step back from the situation at hand and ask yourself: if a cisgender boy and a cisgender girl were engaging in open behavior that some might find objectionable, would I intervene, would I stop them? If your answer is yes, then it is probably appropriate to hold the same standard for any couple. If your answer is no, then deal with your own feelings and leave the youth to theirs.

Consider this example: two youth counselors in a community-based group home were summoned by the other residents to come outside to the front of the group home to see what was going on. When they arrived, they witnessed two of the T/GE residents engaging in simulated sex acts on the group home's front porch. Shocked at first by what they saw, the workers made a quick assessment of the situation and told the young people involved to come inside. They asked the other residents to go back to what they were doing. Although distressed by what the young people were doing on the group home's front porch, they stepped back from the situation, and realized that if a boy and a girl were engaging in this type of behavior, they would know how to address it. They met with both of the young people, individually and then together, to discuss why they were simulating sex. After a discussion about adolescent sexual feelings and expressions of those feelings, the young people said they were bored and that they were just "playing around." They made it clear that they were not involved with one another sexually and they reiterated that they were aware of the house policy that prohibited sexual relationships between residents. The staff asked them to please not "play" like that in public places—particularly in front of the group homes, as they were conscious about being good neighbors. At the house community meeting later that evening, the issue was discussed, not to belittle the youth involved but to stress the importance of appropriate behavior in the community.

In this scenario, a potentially negative situation was turned into a teaching moment by staff who kept their cool and did not allow their own discomfort with the matter at hand to cloud their thinking.

T/GE youth have a right to have relationships and, in fact, dating is a healthy and natural part of their development. Despite the reality that it might make some youth workers and parents/caregivers uncomfortable (Newcomb, Feinstein & Matsion, 2018), it should be nurtured and accepted as a part of all youth's development.

Age-appropriate dating

While it would be most appropriate for youth to be attracted to other youth near their same age, it is possible for young people to be attracted to younger or older people. There are no hard and fast rules for this, except in cases where the young person is clearly under age. However, half your age plus seven is one social rule defining the youngest age one may date without it being socially unacceptable. To compute the oldest one could date without it being socially awkward, simply subtract seven from one's own age, and multiply by two. To compute the acceptable age an otherwise inappropriately matched couple would have to be before they could date, find the difference in their age, multiply by two, and add seven to get the age the older partner would have to be.

Consider the following examples:

Rylan is 23, Skyler is 19. Rylan wants to know if they should date, so he computes half-of-his-age-plus-seven and the result is 18.5 years. This yields, according to the theory, an acceptable relationship.

Reece is 20, Alex is 43. Reece thinks she might be too young for Alex, so she uses the half-the-age-of-Alex-plus-seven rule, and for Alex's age, the result is 28.5 years. According to the theory, this yields an unacceptable relationship.

These examples are just that, examples. Young people should date whoever they choose to date, as long as the relationship is not abusive or fetishized and provided both partners are of legal age. If a young person ever finds themselves in a relationship where they are made to feel they are a sex object due to age, race, gender or sexuality, this should raise a major red flag and the future of the relationship may need to be reconsidered. Every person deserves to be respected and appreciated by their partner, not viewed as an object or prize. It is important to like the person one is dating, not just the idea of them.

At the end of the day, the only people that matter in a relationship are the young person and their partner. How they both choose to conquer these obstacles will determine the outcome of their relationship.

Underage dating

With the rise of social media and dating apps, individuals can be unaware of their partner's age. Some often assume their potential dating partner is above the age of consent based on the way they look, but appearances can be deceiving. Individuals should ask themselves: what are the consequences of engaging in a relationship with an underage young person?

Federal law makes it criminal to engage in a sexual act with another person who is between the ages of 12 and 16 years if they are at least four years younger than you. Each state takes a different approach as the age of consent has ranged from 10 to 18 years. Some states, such as California and New York, set an age under which all sexual intercourse is considered statutory rape. For example, a state might set the age of consent at 18. In this hypothetical state, two 17-year-olds who had consensual sex could both theoretically be convicted of statutory rape.

Other states imply a different method which, like the federal statute, takes into account the relative ages of both people. In these states, such as Texas, the age of consent is determined by age differentials between the two people, limited by a minimum age. For example, a state might set a minimum age of 14 but limit consent to partners who are within three years of their age. This would allow a 16-year-old to lawfully have sex with a 14-year-old, but make it criminal for an 18-year-old to have sex with that same 14-year-old.[1]

1   www.legalmatch.com/law-library/article/statutory-rape-the-age-of-consent.html, downloaded 09/21/2020

Sex between an underage person and an adult

If an adult has sex with someone under the age of consent, they're breaking the law. They could be charged with statutory rape, which means having sex with a person who's under the age of consent, but past the age of puberty. Unlike "forcible rape," statutory rape can mean that the person underage has said yes.

Sexual contact without consent is wrong and illegal whatever the age of the people involved. Young people need to know that if they don't give consent and someone still forces them into having sex, it's never their fault and it's not okay. Young people speak to someone they trust who can assure them that if this has happened they can get help and support.

WHAT CAN YOUTH WORKERS DO?

One thing that all youth workers must ask themselves is: how comfortable am I in dealing with discussions of gender, sexuality and sexual behavior with any youth with whom I work?

Sexuality is a huge part of adolescence. Becoming a sexual being is a major developmental task for all youth. Youth workers may have varying degrees of comfort or discomfort with the topic.

The first step in beginning to examine your feelings about this topic is to be self-reflective on your own values, attitudes and feelings about all forms of sexuality. In some cases, this might mean that youth workers should receive specialized training in human sexuality for T/GE adolescents. Gonzalez (2019) and Langford (2018) are the authors of several wonderful books that address issues of sexuality for T/GE youth.

Youth workers should, as part of this training, also be prepared to have open and accepting conversations with T/GE youth about relationships, sex, intimacy, love, marriage, rearing children, having ceremonies and dating. In essence, T/GE youth desire the same things that all youth hope for. Youth workers should also try not to overreact to the fact that the discussions with T/GE youth will focus on same-gendered, rather than opposite-gendered, expressions.

Youth professionals should be able to define that a healthy relationship comes from respect, mutual understanding, trust, honesty, communication and support, and identify some of the elements of a good relationship. These elements include being able to discuss the benefits of the relationship which has healthy boundaries that are established and respected by both partners equally; acknowledging that a good partner will accept you as you are, support your personal choices and praise you for your achievements; allowing each other to maintain outside interests and friendships; and not hindering the personal freedom of either partner.

In addition to helping the young person to define a healthy relationship, youth workers should be able to do the following when discussing dating issues with T/GE youth:

- Talk openly and realistically about sex and intimacy.

- Talk openly with young people about their dating struggles.

- Make sure that young people know their worth.

- Reiterate that judgmental people are not worthy of their attention.

- Help young people to weather criticism in the dating arena.

- Reiterate that abuse and violence of any type in a relationship should never be tolerated.

- Talk about how and when and if a T/GE young person could disclose their identity in a dating situation.

- Talk openly about the intersectional challenges of race, ethnicity, class, religion, education, ability and geography that these young people might face in the dating arena.

Conclusion

In summary, the ability to be attracted to and date someone is an important step for all youth. Dating clearly has an element of sexual attraction associated with it, but it is also about the ability to develop a healthy relationship with someone to whom you are attracted. Dating is complicated. Dating as a T/GE person adds another layer or two of complications. Rejection is scary on its own, but the addition of being T/GE makes the fear of rejection even scarier. Dating as a T/GE person involves a lot of unknowns, but one thing is for sure, it's an act of brave self-love and resistance to a world that says a person isn't worthy of love just because they're trans. No matter what anyone says, T/GE people deserve love. Everyone deserves to experience all the awkward, fun, cringe-worthy, exciting, infuriating, exciting and blog-worthy dating stories that any cisgender person experiences.

CHAPTER 8

Child Welfare Programs

Most T/GE young people are not placed in child welfare systems. In fact, the majority of T/GE youth live with their families and never rely on a foster home, a group home, a shelter or a child welfare setting at all. Those adolescents who do come to the attention of the child welfare system are young people who have experienced difficulties within their family system to such a degree that they cannot or should not continue to live at home.

Although some T/GE youth are thrown out of their homes when they disclose their gender orientation or gender identity expression or when they are "found out" by their families, not all of them enter child welfare systems because of issues directly related to their gender identity. Like their lesbian, gay, bisexual or cisgender counterparts, the majority of T/GE young people were placed in these systems before or during the onset of adolescence (DeCrescenzo & Mallon, 2000; Mallon & DeCrescenzo, 2017). Some were placed for the same reasons that other young people are placed: family disintegration; divorce, death or physical or mental illness of a parent; parental substance abuse or alcoholism; physical abuse or neglect.

Living apart from one's family is seldom easy. Child welfare systems (foster homes, group homes, congregate care settings and shelters) have long been and continue to be an integral part of youth services systems (see Bullard *et al.*, 2010). The structure of the different types of out-of-home programs varies widely and they can take many forms. They range from family-based foster homes to small community-based group homes and short-term respite care or shelter facilities to large congregate care institutions that provide short-term therapeutic or longer-term custodial care. Some facilities have a juvenile justice component to them (Irvine, 2010; Irvine & Canfield, 2015; Mallon & Perez, 2020), some are family foster care programs (Clements & Rosenwald, 2007), and others still are programs designed for runaway and homeless youth (Maccio & Ferguson, 2016; Shelton, 2015, 2016). All of these different types of services share one common feature, however—they provide care for youth on a 24-hour-a-day basis, which is very different from other youth services that are not residential in nature.

Generally, most group homes, juvenile justice facilities and shelters are staffed by individual youth care workers or counselors who are employed by an agency to work in shifts to cover the facility and provide care for a youth 24 hours a day. The youth care workers who work in group care settings play a very important role in the lives of the young people in their care. Nevertheless, they are generally the lowest paid— and in many cases, have obtained the least education and training—in the youth services system. The daily stress of working with adolescents in these settings, combined with the poor pay, can make it difficult for some staff to be empathetic and compassionate in their dealings with the young people, and these factors also account for a high staff turnover.

Most child welfare care settings for adolescents focus on preparing these young people for transition to adulthood—on or before their 18th birthday, or 21st birthday in some states. Some foster homes, group homes and congregate care settings are warm, loving and accepting of diversity and others are cold, poorly maintained and rigid. T/GE young people live in and speak about both types.

In 2011, the US Administration on Children, Youth and Families (ACYF) Commissioner, Bryan Samuels, issued a memorandum encouraging the protection and support of LGBTQ youth in foster care. The recommended practices elaborate on the provision of services to LGBTQ youth in the areas of foster care, child protection, family preservation, adoption and youth development. They aimed to assist state child welfare agencies to meet the needs of this particularly vulnerable and underserved population by promoting safe, competent and supportive settings for LGBTQ youth and were significant in that the ACYF had never before issued a written policy or offered guidance to support states in working with LGBTQ youth. Despite some changes in policies from the subsequent, more conservative administration, this memorandum stands as the official guidance from the US Department of Health and Human Services (US Department of Health and Human Services, 2011).

T/GE youth in child welfare settings

There have always been T/GE young people in child welfare systems but it has often been difficult for professionals to recognize their existence for three reasons:

1. Many of these young people are invisible to untrained workers.

2. For safety reasons, T/GE young people have learned to hide their identities.

3. Many residential youth services professionals are contemptuous of a T/GE orientation. (Mallon, 1998; Paul, 2018)

In addition, most professionals are completely lacking in knowledge about normative T/GE adolescent development. Additionally, some administrators of child welfare service agencies are fearful that acknowledging a self-identified T/GE young person in their program might be seen as "encouraging" or "promoting" a T/GE identity.

The end result is that T/GE youth often remain hidden and invisible in residential systems, and if they do come out, they are often not provided with the same quality of care that is extended to their cisgender counterparts (Gallegos *et al.*, 2011).

The reflections of one young person about their placement experience is representative of the views of many and provides a framework for examining the salient features of this issue. Tanner is a young person who had several placements in and around a major city in the US:

> My family had many problems. I knew that I was different from the gender I was born into when I was eight years old, and that did cause tension in my family; they just didn't "get" me at all. I came into care because my mother was a substance abuser and didn't take care of us. I went to school hungry, dirty and uncared for. I went to my first foster home when I was 12 years old.

My first foster home was all right, but the family was very religious and they were constantly telling me that I needed to change my ways or I would be condemned—I didn't even know what they meant by that, I was just being myself, but they were not happy with me. I refused to dress the way they wanted me to dress and I insisted that they call me by the name I chose for myself, not the name I was given. After six months, they asked the agency to have me re-placed and I went to a group home for boys. That was horrible! The staff were mean and the kids were just abusive. They called me a "girly boy" and a "shemale" and I was the scapegoat for all that went wrong in that house. I lived in that group home for a year and it was the worst year of my life.

The day when I told my social worker that I couldn't take it any more, my social worker told me that there was this place where I would feel comfortable. She said it was a place for "people like me," a place where I would fit in. I didn't want to go to another group home—the one I was in was bad and I assumed all of them were the same. But, they scheduled a visit for me anyway. It seemed okay when I went on the visit and they transferred me to [the new facility] and I felt comfortable right away. Finally, I had people that I could relate to, people I could talk to. When I first got here, I was so happy—they had this sign that said, "Here, we respect everyone! Regardless of race, religion, sexual orientation, culture, class, gender orientation and ability." I was so relieved; I didn't have to hide nothing from anybody. I could dress the way I wanted to, they called me by the name I chose for myself, they used the correct pronouns, I could walk the way I wanted to, I could be free. I didn't have to hide—I could be myself. It was the first time I had ever felt that way.

Although treatment of T/GE youth in many child welfare systems is improving, stories like Tanner's are not uncommon. T/GE youth, whose circumstances and needs are particularly misunderstood, often suffer especially poor treatment in child welfare systems. They are regularly targeted for harassment and assault, denied necessary medical treatment for their gender dysphoria, given sex-segregated rooming assignments inconsistent with their gender identities, called by their names and personal gender pronouns, and forced to dress in ways that allow no room for their gender expression (Mallon & Perez, 2020). T/GE young people in child welfare systems interviewed for this book reported both positive and negative responses to their gender identity expression, though the negative stories outnumber the positive. Several themes emerge from Tanner's story above and from data collected from narratives provided by other T/GE youth. These themes, discussed below, are useful in understanding the experiences of T/GE youth in residential settings.

Invisibility and hiding

T/GE young people in child welfare systems are frequently an invisible population. This allows administrators and staff to convince themselves that there are no T/GE young people in their care. The majority of T/GE young people are silent and hidden witnesses to the negative attitudes of staff, administrators and peers towards those who workers believe to be T/GE identified. Most T/GE young people in child welfare systems receive—from multiple sources—the message: "Stay in the closet! We do not want to deal with this!"

Stress and isolation

Living in silence, as so many T/GE young people in child welfare systems are forced to do, is the source of a high level of stress and isolation in their lives. The comments of Sawyer exemplify this:

> I tried to hide it because I saw how they treated those kids who they thought were trans. I mean, they were treated terribly—just because the others thought they were trans. I knew that I was trans, so imagine how they would treat me if they ever found out. I felt so alone, so isolated, like no one ever knew the real me. I couldn't talk to anybody about who I was. It was a horrible experience. Trying to hide who you really are is very difficult and exhausting. Sometimes I felt so bad I just wanted to kill myself.

Multiple placements

Moving from one's family to a child welfare setting is, in and of itself, a stressful and traumatic experience. Subsequent moves from one placement to another have been identified as a major difficulty for youth in residential settings. The constant challenge of adapting to a new environment is unsettling, provokes anxiety, and undermines one's sense of permanence. Unlike other cisgender adolescents in residential settings who move from setting to setting because of individual behavioral problems, T/GE youth report that their gender identity expression itself led to multiple and unstable placements, not their behavior.

Young people report experiencing unstable placements for four reasons:

1. They are not accepted because staff have difficulty dealing with their gender identity expression.

2. They feel unsafe due to their gender identity expression and either run away from the placement for their own safety or request new placements.

3. They are perceived as a management problem by staff because they are open about their gender identity expression.

4. They are not accepted by peers due to their gender identity expression.

Tracy provides this narrative which captures their experience of living in a child welfare system:

> I left home at 16 when it was clear that I was T/GE and my family just couldn't support me. They said you can be trans, but you can't live here. They had their own problems with drugs, abuse and all that mess, but somehow I became the punching bag for everyone's issues when I came out as trans. I went to one foster home and that was terrible, because they were worse than my family about my identity. I then went to another foster home and stayed there for a year—it wasn't so bad, because the foster mother just didn't even pay attention to us (there were four other foster kids in that

home) and then the agency winded up closing her home and we had to move again. I then went to a group home and that place was just disgusting—the place was filthy; the staff were plain ignorant about T/GE people and almost everything else. I asked to leave there and I went to another group home—it wasn't so bad and I stayed there for about two years until I aged out. Now, I am on my own—in five years I was in four different places and I guess I was lucky. Lots of T/GE kids that I know were in like 10 or 15 different places.

Many agencies simply get rid of T/GE youth because staff cannot deal with the youth's gender identity expression. Many of these young people have been in multiple placements or been re-placed by agencies at all levels of care. Tanner provides this account:

I have had so many different placements, I can't even remember. Too many to remember...a lot of places. I was 15 when I went to my first one, I've been to lots of them, but I kept running away because I just couldn't live there—the staff just couldn't seem to deal with me. They never called me by my chosen name and they never used the pronoun I asked them to use. They just kept saying "You're gay, right?" and I tried to explain that I was T/GE and not gay, but they just couldn't understand or didn't want to.

These case examples exemplify the ways in which T/GE young people are continuously faced with having to negotiate new environments, many of which are inhospitable and lacking in the conditions necessary for healthy psychological development.

Re-placement and feelings of rejection

The majority of T/GE young people sense that they are not welcome in many of the residential settings where they have been placed. They perceive that they are reluctantly accepted into some placements and consequently feel isolated and have negative reactions to their placement. Many young people are impassioned about their maltreatment in these settings, as this quotation from Carter illustrates:

How was I treated? Oh, God, it was terrible, and it started as soon as I walked into the group home. This staff member, I think she was the supervisor, just pulled me aside and said, "I heard you are gay or T/GE or whatever, and I just want to tell you that you are not gonna do any of that stuff here in this group home." I mean, I wasn't even in the door and they were giving me shit.

When young people are met with acceptance and provided with care that suggests staff are competent in dealing with T/GE youth, they remain in the setting, as Dane notes in this narrative:

Many things fade from my memory as I get older, but the lessons that I learned at GC and the kindness the staff there showed me, the care that they imparted in the most professional way, while still showing that they were human, will never fade. When we lacked a father and a mother our staff were our parents. I can say now that I love myself, I know my self-worth, I value myself and I can have a healthy relationship despite all I went through because the staff in that agency guided me through this time of my life. Thanks to them, I learned to not be afraid of social workers, and while there are good and bad ones, having now seen some good ones, I know there are many more out there that are good than there are bad ones. Thanks to their goodness I was able to feel like a whole person. Today, I am a whole person, if a little cracked in some spots.

Conversely, however, other young people report that they left their placement once they realized that they were not welcomed. Tracy recalls this experience vividly:

I tried to be what they wanted me to be, but I just couldn't. I was who I was, and after six months in that place I thought if I have to stay here I will kill myself. One day, I had just had enough and I thought living in the streets would be better than living in that hell-hole, so I just took my stuff and left. No one even tried to convince me to stay and no one ever came to look for me. I lived with friends, I sofa-surfed and then I found this shelter program that was pretty good and accepted me as I was.

Frequently, young people who leave placements become lost in the system, and their multiple placements create a sense of impermanence and drift.

Verbal harassment and physical violence

Many young people enter foster care because, at its best, it offers sanctuary from abusive family relationships and violence in their homes. However, with the constant threat of harassment and violence within the system, T/GE youth report being unable to feel completely secure or confident (see Mottet & Ohle, 2006). Although violence and harassment may be an unfortunate component of residential care from time to time for all youth, T/GE young people, unlike their cisgender counterparts, are targeted for attack specifically because of their gender identity expression. Petra recalls the nightmare of verbal harassment and physical violence:

> I was coming home to the shelter one night from my job and I was just minding my own business when these three boys from the shelter started to yell at me, "Hey, you she-male, what are you anyway, a guy or a girl?" I tried to ignore them and walked a bit faster to get to the shelter, but they kept following me—taunting me and embarrassing me in front of all of these people on the street. I felt so humiliated, so bad, so low. Finally, one of them jumped me from behind, pulled up my skirt and tried to sexually assault me with his fingers. That's when someone stopped their car and yelled at them to stop. They ran, and this guy got out of his car and asked if I was all right—I said I was because I was embarrassed and humiliated, but I was hurt, inside more than outside. I didn't go back to the shelter that night or any other night. I had some money, so I rented a cheap room for the night and then I went to stay with friends. It was a terrible experience, but I never reported it. I figured no one would do anything about it.

Supporting T/GE youth in child welfare systems

In order to competently serve and safeguard T/GE youth, child welfare staff should understand what it means for a youth to be T/GE and should be familiar with and use appropriate terminology. In addition, child welfare staff should:

- receive mandatory cultural humility training on gender identity and expression, including education regarding social and medical transition issues for T/GE youth diagnosed with gender dysphoria

- have a legal duty to protect the physical and emotional safety of T/GE youth. Child welfare staff should take immediate action to end any form of harassment or bullying against T/GE youth, whether perpetrated by staff, foster parents or peers

- maintain confidentiality regarding the gender identity of T/GE youth in their care and be aware of legal obligations to treat such information confidentially. Staff should not disclose information about a youth's gender identity without first obtaining the youth's permission

- respect a T/GE youth's name and personal gender pronouns that best affirm the young person's gender identity

- allow T/GE youth to express their gender identity through chosen attire, grooming and mannerisms, without punishment or ridicule

- not assume that T/GE youth are "acting out" inappropriately when expressing their gender identity

- not consider or classify youth as sexually aggressive simply because they are T/GE. These young people are no more likely than any others to be sexually aggressive

- avoid making assumptions about the sexual orientation of T/GE youth. T/GE and gender-diverse youth may identify as gay, lesbian, bisexual, questioning, queer, non-binary, asexual or cisgender

- be aware of health care protocols for medical treatment for T/GE individuals and should ensure that T/GE youth have access to competent and trans-affirming mental and medical health services, including access to treatment for gender dysphoria, if deemed medically appropriate. Treatment of gender dysphoria is focused on providing support, not changing a person's gender identity, and may include services such as individual and family counseling and, with a physician's care, hormone therapy and surgery to align the physical body with the gender identity of the youth. Staff should ensure that existing social and medical transition-related treatment is provided after a youth arrives at an agency or facility.

In sex-segregated facilities, T/GE youth should not be designated to the girls' or boys' units strictly based on the sex designated to them at birth. Instead, child welfare staff should make individualized decisions based on the physical and emotional well-being of the youth, considering the young person's wishes, the level of comfort and safety, the degree of privacy afforded, the types of housing available and the recommendations of mental health and medical professionals. The safety of T/GE youth should be protected without resorting to isolating or segregating them from the general population. However, single occupancy rooms, if available in units that correspond with the young person's gender identity, are often appropriate for T/GE youth in sex-segregated facilities.

T/GE youth should be permitted to use the bathrooms that correspond to their gender identity. The facility should counsel others that the youth is entitled to use the bathroom corresponding to the youth's gender identity, and if possible make available private single-person bathrooms as an option. T/GE youth should not be singled out as the only people allowed to use or routed to private single-person bathrooms.

Child welfare staff should support the academic achievements of T/GE youth and ensure that they are safe in schools. The gender expressions of T/GE youth can make them more visible, and therefore more vulnerable, to harassment and violence at school. Some school dress policies make it more difficult for youth to dress consistently with their gender identities.

Child welfare staff should take immediate action to protect T/GE youth facing harassment or discrimination at school, either on-site or off-site, including protecting them from being disciplined for expressing their gender identity or being denied access to locker rooms, showers and bathrooms that match their gender identity.

Child welfare staff should locate and develop resources to help T/GE youth with their legal issues. T/GE youth may need assistance and advocacy to obtain proper legal identity documents reflecting their gender identification and chosen names, such as birth certificates, state identification cards, driver's licenses, health insurance cards, social security cards, passports and school identification cards.

WHAT CAN YOUTH WORKERS DO?

Youth service professionals need to know how to react to the realities that T/GE youth face in child welfare settings. The most important first step is to remember that all youth service professionals have the ethical and moral responsibility to create and maintain safe environments for *every* young person in their care. The establishment of such safety is at the very core of all youth services practice.

Simple solutions cannot be found just by trying to identify T/GE young people. Safe environments grounded in written policies about T/GE youth, practical guidance for staff and ongoing training on the needs of T/GE youth in out-of-home care settings are essential for competent practice and adequate care for T/GE youth residing in such settings (Marksamer, 2011; Wilber, Ryan & Marksamer, 2006).

Conclusion

The problems encountered by T/GE adolescents and their families are frequently ignored and largely unrecognized by the majority of youth services professionals—analogous to the ways in which the youth services system has been deficient in addressing the specific needs of diverse ethnic and racial minorities. An understanding of the impact of societal stigmatization of T/GE individuals and their families is crucial to the recognition of, and response to, the needs of this population.

In addition, youth workers and the systems they work in should consider moving away from residential-style programs and focusing more energy on keeping young people at home, preserving connections with their families of origin, when it is safe to do that, and creating kinship or family-based foster homes for T/GE youth who cannot reside with their families of origin (McCormick, Scheyd & Terrazas, 2017; Salazar *et al.*, 2018).

Effecting changes in attitudes and beliefs in pursuit of competent practice with T/GE adolescents and their families requires education, training and self-exploration on both the individual and institutional level (see Mallon, 2009). The development of competence in this area holds promise for preserving and supporting families and for the establishment of appropriate trans-affirmative out-of-home services for these young people and their families.

CHAPTER 9

Runaway and Homeless Youth Programs

This is Phoenix's story:

> I realized from a very young age about my T/GE identity because I was surrounded by a lot of things in my childhood that forced me to grow up early. I think that is why I began transitioning so young, at age 13. My mother was very religious and a single parent; she couldn't deal with my transition and she kicked me out of the house when she found my clothes and make-up.
>
> I lived with friends for a while on their sofa. But after a while they got tired of me and I had to leave and go to another friend's house. I tried living in group homes and foster homes but that was even worse than living at home. They didn't understand me at all.
>
> I left the last group home, when a staff member tried to sexually assault me. I couldn't take it anymore and I figured that the streets would be safer for me than the group home. I lived in abandoned trucks near the piers with a group of friends that I had met and, to be honest, although that was very sketchy—no bathroom, no running water—it was better than living in the group home. At least the people there cared about me.
>
> After a couple of years of bouncing around, I met this street worker named Jorge from Streetworks and he told me about this shelter that was for kids like me. I didn't believe such a place existed, but I went for a visit at his suggestion and it was a wonderful place. I had to go to an interview and they did have rules, but they totally got T/GE kids and I decided to give it a try. Living on the streets is

hard—I did things to survive that I am not proud of, but I did what I needed to do to get by.

That was about seven years ago. I am now 25 years old, I have a full-time job, I am finishing college and I am finally the person I knew I always knew that I needed to be. Having a roof over my head and support from caring people saved my life.

This chapter addresses issues as they pertain to runaway and homeless youth who identify as T/GE. Homelessness is a critical issue for T/GE people; one in five T/GE individuals have experienced homelessness at some point in their lives. T/GE youth are disproportionately represented in the homeless population (Begun & Kattari, 2015; Shelton, 2015, 2016; Shelton *et al.*, 2017). More generally, some reports indicate that one in five T/GE individuals need or are at risk of needing homeless shelter assistance. However, most homeless shelters for youth are segregated by designated sex, regardless of the individual's gender identity, and homeless T/GE youth are even ostracized by some agencies that serve their LGB peers (Pyne, 2011).

Family rejection and discrimination and violence have contributed to a large number of T/GE youth who are homeless in the US—an estimated 20–40 percent of the more than 1.6 million homeless youth.[1] Social service and homeless shelters that work with this population often fail to culturally and appropriately serve T/GE homeless youth, often denying them shelter based on their gender identity, inappropriately housing them in a gendered space they do not identify with, and failing to address co-occurring issues facing T/GE youth.

Overall, about a third of the nation's 1.4 million T/GE people report experiencing homelessness at some point in their lives. On average, T/GE kids are 13 years old when they first find themselves on the streets. For many T/GE teens, shelter is a misnomer.[2] They often lose beds for minor infractions and are left without recourse for appeal. Shelters have always been unsafe, especially for T/GE and young people.

---

1   https://transequality.org/issues/housing-homelessness, downloaded 05/26/2020

2   https://transequality.org/issues/housing-homelessness, downloaded 05/26/2020

With so few housing options, prostitution is often the easiest way to access a bed.

The precise number of homeless and runaway youth is unknown due to their mobility. Runaway and homeless young people often reject the shelter system for locations or areas that are not easily accessible to shelter workers and others who count the homeless and runaways. Youth who come into contact with census takers may also be reluctant to report that they have left home or are homeless. Determining the number of homeless and runaway youth is further complicated by the lack of a standardized methodology for counting the population and inconsistent definitions of what it means to be homeless or a runaway (Fernandes-Alcantara, 2018).

In one federally funded study, Voices of Youth Count (Morton *et al.*, 2018), researchers used a nationally representative phone survey for national estimates and conducted brief surveys of youth and in-depth interviews of youth who had experiences of homelessness. During a 12-month period, the study interviewed approximately 3.7 percent of households with 13–17-year-olds who explicitly reported homelessness experiences (including running away or being asked to leave). For ages 18–25, household prevalence estimates were 6.7 percent for explicitly reported homelessness. Voices of Youth Count found that approximately 700,000 youth aged 13–17 and 3.5 million young adults aged 18–25 had experienced homelessness within a one-year period.

Family conflict is the primary cause of homelessness for all youth, and this is especially true for T/GE youth. Specifically, familial conflict over a youth's gender identity is a significant factor that leads to homelessness or the need for out-of-home care. According to one study (Mallon, 1998), 50 percent of teens experienced a negative reaction from their parents/caregivers when they came out, and 26 percent were kicked out of their homes. Mallon (1998) further found that more than one third of young people who are homeless or in the care of social services experienced a violent physical assault when they came out, which we know can lead to them leaving a shelter or foster home because, as evidenced by Phoenix's narrative at the start of this chapter, some may actually feel safer on the streets.

Whether T/GE youth are homeless on the streets or in temporary shelter, a review of the available research reveals that they face a multitude of ongoing crises that threaten their chances of becoming healthy, independent adults (Maccio & Ferguson, 2016; Shelton, 2015, 2016; Shelton *et al.*, 2018).

Mental health issues

T/GE homeless youth are especially vulnerable to depression, loneliness and psychosomatic illness, withdrawn behavior, social problems and delinquency.

Several studies (e.g. Mallon, 1998; Paul, 2018) have suggested that more than 50 percent of the runaway and homeless youth populations surveyed identified as lesbian, gay, bisexual or T/GE. Living on the streets puts the health of T/GE youth at constant risk. Runaway and homeless T/GE youth typically do not have ready access to health care that recognizes and addresses sexual concerns. In addition to the life-threatening consequences of HIV infection, substance abuse and street violence, street youth often suffer from upper respiratory infections, body and pubic lice, burns, numerous injuries, sexually transmitted diseases, dermatological problems and mental health issues. The extremes of temperatures, irregular sleep in exposed places, poor diet, propensity toward smoking cigarettes and the lack of opportunities for regular showers exacerbate the problem. Hunger is also a serious issue for street youth.

Homeless T/GE youth are also at risk for severe mental health problems. Street youth suffer primarily from anxiety and depression. Many have also suffered from childhood sexual, physical or emotional abuse or other trauma related to family violence, as evidenced in the following quote from Carter:

> My life didn't start off too well. My mother was drug addicted and left me with my grandmother. When my grandmother died, some family "friend" took me into their home. But life there was terrible— there was all of this sexual, physical and emotional abuse almost every day. It was so bad, but I just thought everybody's life was like that. There were so many people in and out of that house—you never knew who was there. When I came out as T/GE when I was 12 years old, I realized I had to get out of that house—I couldn't take

it anymore. I first lived with some older friends, and then I literally lived on the streets. I stayed in shelters now and then, but basically I learned to take care of myself, because there were no responsible adults in my life.

As evidenced by Carter's account above, at times the psychological stress is more than many young people can endure. Some T/GE youth make suicide attempts to escape from the isolation and estrangement they feel. One youth named Sawyer recalls:

I got high every day. My life was a mess, I hated myself. I had nothing. I didn't have a family that cared for me, I didn't have a home, I didn't have anyone I thought I could go to. I tried to kill myself three times. They always tried at the shelter to give me a referral for counseling, but I never went. I never trusted them. Finally, after a pretty serious suicide attempt—I took a bunch of pills—I was hospitalized. When I was released from the hospital they found me a good place to stay and things have been better since then.

Substance abuse

The combination of stressors inherent to the daily life of homeless youth leads them to abuse drugs and alcohol. It has been estimated that between 10 and 20 percent of homeless youth self-identify as chemically dependent (Gower *et al.*, 2018; Morton, 2020).

These risks are exacerbated for homeless youth identifying as T/GE. Personal drug usage, family drug usage and the likelihood of enrolling in a treatment program are all higher for T/GE homeless youth than for their cisgender peers.

Risky sexual behavior

All homeless youth are especially vulnerable to engaging in risky sexual behaviors because their basic needs for food and shelter are not being met. Defined as "exchanging sex for anything needed, including money, food, clothes, a place to stay or drugs," survival sex is the last resort for many T/GE homeless youth (Kattari & Begun, 2017, p.96). A study of homeless youth in Canada (Abramovich, 2016; Abramovich & Shelton, 2017) found that those who identify as T/GE were three times more likely to participate in survival sex than their heterosexual peers, and 50 percent of homeless youth in another study (Freeman & Hamilton, 2008) considered it likely or very likely that they would someday test positive for HIV.

Lauren is a former "system kid" who has lived on the streets of New Orleans for many years. Their story illustrates many of the risks for T/GE street youth:

> When I was about nine years old I went into foster care placement. My mother was an alcoholic and heroin user. She neglected us a lot and a lot of the neighbors saw that and there was a lot of complaints made, and so the DCFS [Department of Children and Family Services] ended up coming to the house and finding my mother not there, or going there and finding my mother there but she was high and the house a mess, you know, or finding drug paraphernalia. We were dirty, never went to school, you know, so we were placed in foster care. We were taken in and out of foster homes a lot, taken away, then given back to my mother, four months in, then given back, three months in and then given back, a week in and then given back. As we got older it progressed, it got worse. I mean, we went from going to foster homes to going to group homes. I got into trouble, shoplifting, assaulting people, and they sent me to juvenile detention.
>
> I was about 17 when I was released and that's when I hit the streets. I couldn't go home—didn't have a home, they didn't want me back in the group homes and I just kinda started to hang out, you know, staying at friends' houses. Finally I started to just spend more and more time on the streets in the Quarter. I spent a few nights in Covenant House on Rampart, but then I'd either get fed up with the rules or kicked out for getting into conflicts with other residents. To be honest, it didn't always have to do with my sexuality—I worked in clubs down on St. Anns. I am trans, so I attracted a lot of attention.
>
> I started to like a lot of the things I found out on the street and in the clubs. I mean, I started hustling at that point, you know prostitution—I was into guys and girls. I thought that I wasn't going to be able to get into this, then I ended up liking it you know and

getting into it. I made a lot of money. But I also got into drugs big time—coke, heroin, hard stuff. Prostitution is more about drugs than sex in some ways. I did it all out there. About two months ago I took the HIV test, and found out that I'm HIV positive. Sometimes folks in the drop-in center I go to try to help me get it together and there's times when I'd like to get it together, you know, to have a home, but then I think...maybe it's too late for me.

Victimization of runaway and homeless youth

T/GE youth face the threat of victimization in many arenas: at home, at school, at their jobs and, for those who are out-of-home, at shelters and on the streets. T/GE homeless youth are more likely than their cisgender peers to be victims of a crime.[3] While some public safety agencies try to help this vulnerable population, others adopt a "blame the victim" approach, further decreasing the odds of victimized youth feeling safe in reporting their experiences.

Services for T/GE runaway and homeless youth

Although T/GE street youth have some unique service provision needs, most require the same services as their cisgender or LGB counterparts. Among the services that street youth require are: direct services on the street; drop-in centers; and shelter and transitional living programs.

Direct services on the street

Life on the streets is a transient and shifting scene. Before programs are initiated, workers must survey the street scene to determine the "turf"—to find out who hangs out where. Although there is blending, T/GE street kids hang out in different areas in different cities from cisgender street youth. In urban areas, street work begins by visiting youth-oriented gathering areas: parks, street corners, "strolls" (areas where some T/GE youth are known to solicit sex for survival), and

---

3   www.hrc.org/resources/violence-against-the-T/GE-community-in-2019, downloaded 05/25/2020

specific neighborhoods, restaurants which are tolerant of T/GE life and where T/GE youth are known to hang out. Youth may also hang out around bus or train terminals in the area because they are open late at night. Fast-food restaurants and some coffee shops in these areas also have late-night hours and may attract street youth. Peep shows, bars, nightclubs and transient hotels in these areas also are places where T/GE street youth may congregate. In rural and suburban areas, youth hang out in different ways. For example, in rural farming areas, homeless youth hang out in corn fields, where they are not observed.

Street workers need to assess their safety levels on the street. Two-person teams are ideal. They create a partnership so that workers feel less isolated. Although safety is paramount, hanging out regularly is the first step to becoming part of the street scene.

In some areas, T/GE street youth may seem invisible and indistinguishable from other street youth. However, when this group is observed by workers who are knowledgeable about T/GE people, they can be differentiated from the others.

Most importantly, street workers must learn to listen to youth. Young people who live on the streets have a very low level of trust in adults; many have been used by adults and trust will have to be earned. Although written decades ago, Able-Peterson and Bucy's (1993) guidelines continue to offer several rules for engaging homeless youth:

Rule 1: First and foremost, street workers must learn young people's names. Young people feel important when someone has taken the time to connect and learn their names. Use whatever name they give you— street youth use nicknames regularly. Do not press them to disclose their designated name with you in the earliest stages of a developing relationship. It is also important to repeat *your* name to them every time you see them, so that they will get used to hearing and using yours. A person is not a stranger if they are using first names. It is also important to remember that every new person is viewed with suspicion.

Rule 2: It is essential that street workers state very simply who they are, and with whom they are connected. In working with T/GE street youth, workers must be especially attuned to their unique culture and language. Many workers carry cards with their names and their agency's name and services printed on them. Cards distributed should refer to services which are specific to T/GE youth. Introductory assessment questions should be utilized in a conversational manner. Stress food, clothing, showers and medical care. Repeat your name and theirs when you say goodbye.

Rule 3: Street workers need to be patient and consistent. Engagement and relationship building with street youth takes time. Young people who have survived on the streets know that it was their wariness that has kept them alive. Street workers need to be clear that what they offer (food, clothing, shelter) comes with no strings attached. Although trust is developed slowly, there is an easy camaraderie on the streets. After a worker has bumped into a youth three or four times, they begin to get used to the worker's presence and may begin to form a relationship with him or her.

Rule 4: Workers need to trust the process. There are no short cuts to relationship building. As the relationship develops between the youth and the street worker, so usually will the requests for assistance. Case management, resource identification and advocacy often begin on the streets, but may move into the drop-in center as time, need and the relationship progresses.

Drop-in centers

Drop-in centers provide a transition from the work conducted on the streets to longer-term services. They are places where youth can take a shower, do laundry, get clothes, meet with a counselor, attend a life skills group, participate in a GED class, take part in a recreational activity, have a meal, and begin to deepen relationships. Drop-in centers are usually located near areas where youth hang out. Some centers also have medical vans attached to their programs and provide much-needed health care for youth on the streets. T/GE youth who have spent a great deal of time on the streets might be initially reluctant to participate in drop-in center activities because of past negative experiences with insensitive social services providers. Peer outreach is key to ensuring that the center is a safe place for all youth.

Shelters and transitional living programs

Since 1974, shelters have been an important part of the array of services available to street youth. T/GE youth, many of whom have experienced very poor fits in the child welfare system, might avoid shelters or transitional living programs at all costs (Abramovich, 2016; Cray, Miller & Durso, 2013). Although family reunification is a major impetus, such goals, without a true understanding of the needs of street youth, are evidence of how little policy-makers understand the reasons why many T/GE young people flee from their homes. Reunification may be possible for many homeless young people, but for others, it must be acknowledged that it is not a realistic or practical goal. It is important to realize that crisis intervention and residential care for young people whose separation from their family will become permanent is very different from interventions with first-time runners. In most cases, individual host homes, rather than a shelter, may be a preferable alternative for less street-wise youth.

T/GE homeless youth often are especially unsafe at shelters that assign them beds according to their sex designated at birth and not their gender identity. These insensitive shelter policies may cause a T/GE youth who identifies as female to be placed in a male facility, where she is at increased risk of abuse and rape. Furthermore, sex-segregated bathrooms, locker rooms and dressing areas within these facilities are often inappropriate and unsafe for T/GE youth. T/GE youth who are unsafe in shelters are more likely to run away. On the streets, they frequently find a thriving, often dangerous underground market for hormones and other medical procedures as they seek to align their physical bodies with their gender identities.

Shelters and host homes that are committed to providing care for T/GE youth must consciously focus on creating an affirming and supportive environment to ensure safety for all young people. At the very minimum, shelter staff and host-home volunteers, at all levels, should be knowledgeable and trained about T/GE culture and norms, including use of a young person's affirmed name and personal gender pronouns. Agency literature should include specific references to welcoming and working with T/GE people, and health and mental health care providers must be able to "send out cues" through their language and by their actions that they are comfortable with, confident in and knowledgeable about working with T/GE youth. Shelters that do not create an affirming environment for T/GE youth will not be utilized by them.

Transitional living programs (TLPs), funded by the Family and Youth Services Bureau, are usually single apartments rented by multi-service youth-serving organizations in the community to house homeless youth. TLPs are excellent program models for adolescents who are moving toward self-sufficiency. In addition to providing stable, safe living accommodations while a homeless youth is a program participant, these programs also provide an array of services necessary to assist homeless youth in developing both the skills and personal characteristics needed to enable them to live independently. Among these services are education, life skills development, information and counseling aimed at preventing, treating and reducing substance abuse among homeless youth, and appropriate referrals and access to medical and mental health treatment. Youth may live in these supervised living arrangements for up to 18 months.

Conclusion

Like adult homelessness, T/GE youth homelessness is not simply a matter of identifying housing for a young person. Nor should youth homelessness be viewed entirely as an indicator of problem youth behavior, but as evidence of society's inability to develop adequate supports for youth and families troubled by economic hardship, substance abuse, sexual orientation and/or gender identity issues, incest and familial violence. All runaway and homeless youth face a multitude of problems when on the streets. T/GE youth are further burdened by lack of family support, unsafe child welfare placements, cisgenderism and transphobia. The dual stigmatization of being T/GE and homeless can lead to an overwhelming sense of despair and hopelessness. Making mainstream runaway and homeless youth services accessible to T/GE youth is an active, ongoing and evolving process that requires organizational sensitivity and responsiveness. Homeless T/GE youth can be moved from the streets into appropriate homes if they are provided with competent practitioners to work with them and programs designed to sensitively meet their needs.

CHAPTER 10

A Call for Organizational Transformation

Over the past few years, several authors (Brill & Kenney, 2016; Mallon, 2009; Mallon & Perez, 2020; Nealy, 2019; Shelton, 2015) have enumerated the needs of T/GE youth and identified the obstacles that youth-serving agencies face in addressing these needs. This final chapter, utilizing the experiences of several nationally known T/GE affirming agencies, offers recommendations on agency philosophies concerning the reality of T/GE youth. It also offers suggestions on ways to create safe, welcoming and nurturing environments.

The dilemmas faced by T/GE youth and their families are clear. Youth-serving agencies, already challenged by many substantial issues, tend to exhibit a range of sensitivities to T/GE youth. At one extreme, some agencies openly discriminate against T/GE youth; at the other end of the spectrum, agencies are affirming in their approaches and strongly advocate for their needs. Most youth-serving agencies fall somewhere in the middle. Many agencies initiate good faith efforts to become more affirming, but this usually occurs when they come across their first openly T/GE youth. A more proactive stance, and preparation for working with diverse groups of young people, rarely happens without a precipitating incident.

Youth-serving agencies come into contact with T/GE youth for several reasons: family conflict, health or mental health of the youth, school problems, recreation, or child welfare placements. The scope of these issues, as reviewed in this book, requires that all youth-serving agencies become knowledgeable about and sensitive to the needs of T/GE youth. The vulnerability of T/GE youth, particularly at times when they come to the attention of youth-serving agencies, is yet another reason that youth providers should be prepared for working with this population. The most inopportune time to increase one's knowledge about a service population is when they arrive at the agency in a crisis and are in need of immediate assistance.

Efforts to increase sensitivity to T/GE youth cannot be sustained in an environment that does not explicitly encourage such undertakings. As agencies struggle to demonstrate their commitment to diversity and inclusion, they must also be willing to include gender identity expression in that diversity/inclusion continuum. In doing so, they begin the work necessary for creating a safe and welcoming environment for all young people, not just T/GE youth. Once this orientation is set, and the organization's culture shifts to clearly include T/GE concerns, it becomes possible for youth workers to learn about, advocate for and provide affirming services to T/GE youth.

While it is a reality that some agency administrators and boards might object to specific T/GE sensitivity awareness or programs particularly geared toward the population, fewer should take exception to overall approaches designed to increase worker competence in working with youths who are underserved.

Transforming the organization's culture

Transformation is a powerful word, but nothing less is needed to create programs that are responsive to the needs of T/GE youth. Appreciation of diversity and inclusion is a key element in this process. The examination of an organization's commitment to diversity and inclusion is a common theme for all youth-serving agency administrators. Diversity and inclusion approaches in organizations have utilized various strategies to increase worker competence and cultural humility in meeting the needs of a varied youth population, including in-service training, non-discrimination policies, culturally specific celebrations, advocacy, youth/staff groups that explore diversity and inclusion, and efforts to encourage a climate that welcomes all people. A T/GE approach could be integrated into any one of these areas. A community-based youth center commemorating Latinx History Month with a potluck dinner representing dishes from various Latinx countries could just as easily celebrate T/GE Awareness Week. This is typically observed during the second week of November and is a one-week celebration leading up to T/GE Day of Awareness, which memorializes victims of transphobic violence by inviting a speaker to discuss the events that led to the civil rights struggle for the T/GE community.

Youth-oriented agencies must also be committed to creating safe environments for all youth. The enactment of a zero-tolerance policy for violence, weapons, emotional maltreatment, slurs of all types and direct or indirect mistreatment conveys to all youths that their safety is a priority. A strong stance against violence of all types, including verbal harassment, sends an important message to all youth. It says, "We will protect you and you will not be blamed for being yourself. Those who offend are the ones who will be dealt with, because their behavior is unjustified and unacceptable."

All youth benefit from youth workers who are open, honest and genuine. Everyone benefits from philosophies that indicate an agency's willingness to address difficult issues head on. Giving youth and staff permission to raise controversial topics signals that all people associated with the agency will be treated with respect and dignity.

It is only through intentional and deliberate organizational cultural and inclusive shifts—true transformation—that a climate supportive of T/GE youth can be developed. Several agencies across the US and internationally have been successful in creating organizations where T/GE youth are welcomed, feel safe and have their needs met. This does not take huge amounts of money, tremendous time commitments on the part of staff, or other extraordinary efforts. It does, however, need commitment from board members, administrators and other key organizational players, including the youth and their families. There is no need to start this process from scratch, as there are several excellent resources that could be adapted to meet your organization's needs.[1]

What follows are concrete strategies that organizations may consider when actively working towards transforming their workplace environments.

---

1   See www.thehrcfoundation.org/professional-resources/trans-toolkit-for-employers

Concrete strategies
Hiring supportive employees

An organization that is responsive to the needs of T/GE youth must be staffed and administered by people who demonstrate a similar commitment to providing services that foster self-esteem and acceptance for T/GE youth. To achieve this, the organization must aim to hire open-minded, supportive employees, including openly T/GE professionals. Organizations must communicate anti-discrimination policies in hiring, and must be honest about recruiting and maintaining gender-expansive employees. Hiring openly T/GE employees sends a clear message that the agency is demonstrating its commitment to T/GE youth. Although hiring T/GE staff is critical, it should not be assumed that every T/GE person is knowledgeable about working with T/GE youth, or appropriate for working with them. All staff, regardless of gender identity expression, should be assessed for their appropriateness in working with youth, and then educated about T/GE youth, the problems that they experience in society and how to effectively support them. Hiring cisgender staff and LGB staff that are comfortable with T/GE youths and open to being educated about working with this population is also an essential part of this process.

With increasing openness about gender identity expression, youths often ask employees about their gender identity expression. Some youth-serving agencies have encouraged staff to be open about their gender orientation, because ambiguity about a staff member's orientation can lead to mistrust in the youth. Once staff are clear, youth stop playing guessing games and start to do the work that they have come to the agency for in the first place.

One of the most positive outcomes of recruiting openly T/GE staff reported by several of the agencies was that staff turnover was at an all-time low. Being employed in an accepting atmosphere is a great employee benefit for T/GE adults.

In-service and ongoing training

In-service and ongoing training, integrated into the overall training efforts of the organization, is critical in providing quality services to T/GE youth and families. As with all issues of diversity and inclusion efforts, integrating real-life case examples into the training sessions can make the educational process come alive for workers. Helping staff to identify appropriate language and personal gender pronoun usage, addressing the common myths and stereotypes that most people have about T/GE people, replacing the myths with accurate information about the population, and creating environments that suggest safety— these are all good first steps. However, training efforts should be tailored to meet the individual needs of staff members from various disciplines (see Elze & McHaelen, 2009; Fox, 2019; Ruggs *et al.*, 2015).[2]

Helping staff to identify resources in the community and to assess their own personal transphobia are also critical factors in the training process. Use of videos and guest speakers, especially T/GE youth or their parents/caregivers, can be particularly effective in getting the message across.

Transferring abstract information learned in training sessions into actual intervention techniques takes practice. Participation in a variety of exercises assists staff members in beginning to develop a set of appropriate and unconstrained responses. Opportunities should be created where staff members are intentionally exposed to situations that lead to self-reflection. For example, in one training session focusing on the maladaptive coping responses that can be associated with hiding one's gender identity expression, the participants were asked at the start of the session to write their most personal secret on a slip of paper, to fold it, and to place it under the chair that they would be sitting on all day. Without ever being asked to share what they wrote, the message was powerful. In the ensuing discussion, attitudinal change and understanding of the consequences of secrecy could begin to evolve.

Providing staff at the training sessions with written information, resources and other materials ensures that the educational process continues after the training session is finished. This process should be monitored and evaluated by program supervisory staff.

---

2   www.transgendertraininginstitute.com

Welcoming strategies

The creation of a physical environment that welcomes T/GE youth, families and prospective employees is as significant as staff training. Again, these efforts do not need to cost a great deal of money, but evidence of them signals acceptance and safety.

The organization's waiting room is probably the most important place to start this process. Reading materials, symbols and signs that specifically spell out the organization's attitude about respect for all people will be noticed and will help youths, their families and employment applicants feel welcome.

Many agencies have posters hung in their waiting rooms that signal acceptance. One agency in New York specifically developed nine colorful, gender-neutral posters that proclaim a T/GE-affirming environment. The messages that these send are intentionally subtle. T/GE organizations will also be able to provide organizations with pamphlets; others can be downloaded from the internet. Even religiously affiliated organizations can hang up these posters.

The presence or lack of books focusing on T/GE issues also conveys important messages. For a comprehensive list of books on a variety of topics pertinent to T/GE youth see the resources listed in Appendix B. Thousands of T/GE-related books might also be purchased in bookstores and online.

Integrated policies and public information materials

Although T/GE people have experienced greater acceptance and understanding in the past decades, many organizations may still actively discriminate against T/GE youth. In other cases, the organization's inattentiveness to the needs of T/GE youth will send a clear signal that they are not welcome. A review of the organization's policies and public materials can assist the organization in consistently attempting to provide sensitive services to all youth.

An organization's commitment to T/GE youth involves more than posters and books. It is critical to recognize that the internal structure of the organization, as reflected in its policies and public information materials, may also need to be evaluated. Training and educational efforts may assist staff in developing their competence in working with a particular population, but policies and what the outside community knows about the organization may also need to be altered in order to effect real change.

Advocacy efforts

Recognizing that the environment outside the organization is often actively hostile to T/GE youth, youth-serving agencies must also be committed to external change and advocacy efforts as well. This may mean participating in an advocacy campaign to end discriminatory language in contracts and/or attending human services-related conferences. Affirming organizations must also be prepared to advocate for T/GE youth in community schools, in local adolescent treatment settings, and in families. Further, organizational leaders must also be prepared to educate local and state politicians and funders about the needs of T/GE youth.

As the 21st century progresses, youth workers continue to play a critical role in developing young people. Youth work has historically had a cyclical interest in certain subjects: youth suicide, violence, substance abuse and homelessness. All are worthwhile issues that require our best efforts, but the needs of T/GE youth should not be viewed as the "issue du jour" of youth work. Issues of gender identity expression are too vital to continue to be overlooked. A particular T/GE youth might trigger a plethora of attention at the time, only to fade from view when the next issue presents itself. Dealing with T/GE youth issues in an intermittent manner is a mistake. Organizations must continue to diligently develop training, assess their own ability or inability to respond to the needs of T/GE youth and address new approaches to competent practice with these young people and their families. For an organization to be consistently sensitive to the needs of its young people, efforts to create affirming environments and to transform existing ones must be realized. If organizations are guided by the same principles that embrace diversity and inclusion and can translate these into concrete action, T/GE youth will be better served.

However, regardless of the organizational changes that must occur, the most powerful influence in a young person's life is the individual contact, and the ability to form a relationship with a competent and caring youth worker. While the organizational structure can set the stage for a T/GE-affirming environment where a young T/GE person can socialize, learn and find a safe place to be themselves, it is the individual youth worker with whom they will engage and connect, and possibly disclose the most personal information to.

It is my hope that this book has offered some useful guidance to those youth workers who are truly trying to do their best for all the young people with whom they work.

Appendix A: Explanation of Terms: A Glossary for Child Welfare Practitioners

As with any youth-oriented culture, T/GE youth have their own unique language, and an ability to speak their language is essential. The language of T/GE youth makes many adults uncomfortable, but to be effective in working with them, adults must overcome their discomfort and become familiar with the terms that T/GE youth use to define themselves. Workers may also want to utilize online slang dictionaries (i.e. Urbandictionary.com), which cover both complimentary and offensive terms, to keep up with the ever-changing lexicon. Listed below are several key terms that will assist youth workers in building their competency in working with T/GE youth.

This glossary is intended to orient the reader to the more commonly used vocabulary in T/GE literature, culture and speech. Language is often a source of confusion and misinformation and, as such, it is important that service providers have accurate definitions. Many heterosexually oriented care providers are often unfamiliar and uncomfortable with the vernacular of the T/GE culture. It should be recognized that, as with any subculture—particularly oppressed groups—there is a constantly changing argot. Usage may vary with generation, geography, socio-economic status and racial, ethnic or cultural background.

It should also be noted that T/GE youth first coming to terms with their gender identity expression may not use these terms to define themselves—they might say, "I feel different," "I feel like sometimes I was born in the wrong body" or "I have a girl body, but a boy brain." The following terms should also never be used for youth just coming to terms with their identities in a direct question, such as: "Are you trans?" or "Are you someone struggling with gender?" But with this in mind, professionals need to know what the appropriate terms in the 21st century are and be able to use them comfortably in working with T/GE youth.

The language in this publication is intended to be understandable and acceptable. The terms specifically utilized by lesbian, gay, bisexual and questioning youth will not be explored herein, as they have been fully discussed elsewhere (Mallon, 2017). While no one owns definitions, many of the definitions below are based on previous work developed by Mallon (2017) and others.[1]

Terminology

Language is often a source of confusion and misinformation and, as such, it is important that service providers have accurate definitions. Cisgender-oriented practitioners are often unfamiliar or uncomfortable with the vernacular of the T/GE "culture." In addition, one must understand the differences between sexual orientation issues and gender identity expression—they are not the same, and although professionals are quick to lump lesbian, gay, bisexual and questioning youth with T/GE youth, the differences between sexual orientation and gender identity expression as well as between each identity are extensive. It should also be acknowledged that as with any subculture— particularly that of oppressed groups—language used by others, but more importantly by those with lived experiences, is constantly changing. Usage may vary with different generations, geographic areas of the world, socio-economic status and racial, ethnic or cultural backgrounds. Which terms are acceptable and which are offensive varies widely and is also culturally dependent.

Affirmed gender: The process of bringing the gender role and appearance into alignment with the gender identity, which "affirms" that identity. Thus, the term "affirmed" gender is now becoming more common in describing an individual's gender status.

Agender individuals: An individual who identifies as genderless or gender neutral.

Ally: Any person who actively supports LGBTQA (lesbian, gay, bisexual, T/GE, queer or asexual) individuals and causes, and speaks out in support of justice for LGBTQA communities.

---

[1]   www.lgbthealtheducation.org, downloaded 02/18/2020; https://lgbtqia.ucdavis. edu, downloaded 02/18/2020

Androgyny: The mixing of masculine and feminine gender expression or the lack of gender identification. The terms *androgyne*, *agender* and *neutrois* are sometimes used by people who identify as genderless, non-gendered, beyond or between genders, or some combination of these.

Asexual: An individual who has a lack of sexual attraction to others, or low or absent interest in or desire for sexual activity.

Ball culture: Emerged initially in the 1920s in and around New York City. To begin with, performers consisted mainly of white men putting on drag fashion shows. Because of racist attitudes, black queens rarely participated, and established their own ball culture in the 1960s. The 1970s saw an expansion of ball participation as balls increased their numbers and types of categories to allow inclusivity and involvement of everyone. Balls became a safe space for youth of color, mainly blacks and Latinos/Latinas, to express themselves freely. See also *Paris is Burning* (Livingston, 1990), which documents New York City ballroom culture in the late 1980s, and *Pose* (Murphy, Falchuk & Canals, 2018), a 2018 TV show focusing on the ball scene in 1987 and 1993.

Bigender: Refers to those who identify as two genders. Can also identify as multigender (identifying as two or more genders). Do not confuse this term with two-spirit, which is specifically associated with Native American and First Nations cultures.

Bottom surgery: Genital-affirming surgeries such as vaginoplasty, phalloplasty and metoidioplasty.

Breast augmentation: Enlarging one's breasts using breast implants, not for cosmetic reasons, but to address one's gender dysphoria.

Chest binding: A way for many T/GE men to curb dysphoria. It is also a fairly common step in T/GE feminine transition. "Binding" refers to flattening breast tissue to create a male-appearing chest using a variety of materials and methods. While binding with common household items is an inexpensive route, it can also be unsafe; using a chest binder is a safer alternative.

Chest masculinization: A bilateral mastectomy that removes most of the breast tissue, shapes a contoured male chest, and refines the nipples and areolas.

Cisgender: A gender identity that Western society considers to "match" the biological sex designated at birth. The prefix cis- means "on this side of" or "not across from." The term is used to call attention to the privilege of people who are not T/GE.

Coming out as T/GE: Coming out as T/GE may mean that one tells people about one's personal gender pronouns (if one wishes to be referred to as he/him/his, she/her/hers or they/them/their). It may also mean that one asks to be called by a chosen name and to be identified by their affirmed gender identity. Coming out as T/GE is a very personal decision and different for everyone. Some people choose to come out before they medically or socially transition, and some choose to come out after or during the process. One may choose to come out to different people at different times, or to not come out to some people at all. All of this is okay—only the T/GE individual can decide what's right for them. Although all involve telling friends and family about one's identity, there are differences between coming out as lesbian, gay or bisexual and coming out as T/GE.

Cross-dressing: Dressing as the other gender for entertainment or pleasure. Cross-dressing isn't necessarily a sign of a person's gender identity or sexual orientation. Cross-dressing also isn't indicative of gender dysphoria.

Dead name: The birth name of somebody who has changed their name. Most commonly attributed to T/GE people.

Deadnaming: Occurs when someone, intentionally or not, refers to a person who is T/GE by the name they used before they transitioned. It may also be described as referring to someone by their "birth name" or their "given name."

Designated sex at birth: At the time of birth, most infants are categorized as either male or female. This is usually based on the appearance of their external genitalia, although it can be more complicated in some cases. Designated sex at birth, or recorded sex at birth, refers to the determination of whether infants' bodies appear to be male or female. It is this sex that is recorded on the birth certificate.

Drag or in drag: The term drag queen originates in Polari, the language of gay men in England in the early part of the last century. Drag meant clothes, and was also theatre slang for a woman's costume worn by a male actor. Drag is a part of Western gay culture—it involves wearing exaggerated and sometimes outrageous costumes or imitating movie and music stars of the opposite sex. It is a form of performance art practiced by drag queens and kings. Female-bodied people who perform in usually exaggerated men's clothes and personae are called drag kings, though this term has a wider meaning than drag queen. Drag kings should not just be seen as female equivalents of drag queens, because the term covers a much wider field of gender performance and political activism. Gender identity among drag kings is far more varied, too. Drag kings are largely a phenomenon of lesbian culture; they have only recently begun to gain the fame or focus that drag queens have known for years (see also Charles, 2018).

Facial feminization surgery: Includes such procedures as reshaping the nose, and brow or forehead lift; reshaping of the chin, cheek and jaw; Adam's apple reduction; lip augmentation; hairline restoration; and earlobe reduction.

Facial masculinization surgery: Includes such procedures as forehead lengthening and augmentation; cheek augmentation, reshaping the nose and chin; jaw augmentation; and thyroid cartilage enhancement to construct an Adam's apple.

Female-affirmed: Describes someone who was designated a male gender identity at birth but who identifies as female.

Female-to-male (FTM): Indicates a T/GE individual who was originally designated the sex of a female at birth, but has claimed a male identity through clothing, surgery, hormones and/or attitude changes. *This is a term that some but not all transgender people use.*

Gender: That which a society deems "masculine" or "feminine." Gender is socially constructed and is not necessarily the same as an individual's biological sex.

Gender-affirming surgery: Surgical procedures that change one's body to conform to one's gender identity. Gender-affirming surgery is sometimes referred to as gender-reassignment surgery or gender-confirming surgery.

Gender dysphoria: A clinical symptom that is characterized by a sense of alienation to some or all of the physical characteristics or social roles of one's designated gender; also, gender dysphoria is the psychiatric diagnosis in the *DSM-5*, which has focus on the distress that stems from the incongruence between one's expressed or experienced (affirmed) gender and the gender assigned at birth. This diagnosis replaced gender identity disorder in the *DSM-5*.

Gender expression: Refers to the ways in which people externally communicate their gender identity to others through behavior, clothing, hairstyles, voice and other forms of presentation. Gender expression also works the other way as people assign gender to others based on their appearance, mannerisms and other gendered characteristics. Gender expression should not be viewed as an indication of sexual orientation.

Gender fluidity: This is the exhibition of a variability of gender identity and expression. Gender fluid people don't feel restricted by typical societal norms and expectations and might identify and express themselves as masculine, feminine or along a spectrum, and possibly with variations over time (see Diamond, 2008).

Gender identity: The individual internal concept of self in terms of female, male, non-binary or gender expansive (a blend, neither, both or more than we have language for). Gender identity is in an internal working model for how the gender(s) of a person relates to the world at large, and it does not need to be reflected or justified by social, medical and political structures. Gender identity may match or be different from sex designated at birth.

Genderqueer: A rejection of the male/female gender binary in favor of a more fluid, non-traditional identity.

Gender role: Refers to the sets of activities, thoughts, emotions and/or behaviors traditionally considered "normative" for men or women within a culture.

Gender variant: Displaying gender traits that are not normatively associated with their biological sex. "Feminine" behavior or appearance in a male is gender variant as is "masculine" behavior or appearance a female. Gender-variant behavior is culturally specific (see Drescher & Pula, 2014).

Genital tucking: A practice employed by some T/GE women and gender-diverse individuals to minimize or hide the contour (bulge) of their genitals, creating a flatter and more feminine appearance. For many people, tucking is immensely helpful in relieving gender dysphoria and allowing them to wear clothing that affirms their gender. There are a wide variety of methods used to tuck, involving the use of athletic tape, tight underwear and specialized supportive undergarments called gaffs.

Hormone replacement therapy (HRT): The process in which T/GE people choose to take a prescription of synthetic hormones. For T/GE women, that may include estrogen as well as testosterone blockers. For T/GE men it is testosterone (T).

Internalized oppression: The belief that cisgender people are "normal" or better than T/GE people, as well as the often-unconscious belief that negative stereotypes about T/GE people are true.

Intersex: Having hormones, chromosomes and/or primary sexual characteristics, including genitalia and/or internal sex organs, that are different from what is typically considered to be biologically male or female. This is not the same as the term "hermaphrodite," which is an antiquated and offensive term to intersex folks and their allies.

Male-affirmed: Describes someone designated a female gender identity at birth but who identifies as male.

Male-to-female (MTF): A T/GE individual who was originally designated the sex of male at birth, but has claimed a female identity through clothing, surgery, hormones and/or attitude changes. *This is a term that some but not all T/GE people use.*

Metoidioplasty: A surgical procedure that works with the existing genital tissue of the clitoris to form a phallus, or new penis. It can be performed on anyone with significant clitoral growth caused by using testosterone.

Misgendering: When someone intentionally or unintentionally refers to a person, relates to a person, or uses language to describe a person that doesn't align with their affirmed gender.

Non-binary: Some people have a gender which is neither male nor female and may identify as both male and female at one time, as different genders at different times, as no gender at all, or dispute the very idea of only two genders. Such gender identities outside the binary of female and male are increasingly being recognized in legal, medical and psychological systems and diagnostic classifications in line with the emerging presence and advocacy of these groups of people. In recent years, a growing number of T/GE individuals have identified as non-binary rather than as the other binary gender.

Pangender and polygender: An individual who affirms a gender identity that encompasses more than female and male genders.

Pansexual: An individual who feels love and sexual attraction towards others without placing importance on the partner's sex or gender—people, not parts.

Penile construction/phalloplasty: The construction of a penis generally includes several procedures that are often performed in tandem. These may include: a hysterectomy to remove the uterus, an oophorectomy to remove the ovaries, a vaginectomy to remove the vagina, a phalloplasty to turn a flap of donor skin into a phallus, a scrotectomy to turn the labia majora into a scrotum, a urethroplasty to lengthen and hook up the urethra inside the new phallus, a glansplasty to sculpt the appearance of an uncircumcised penis tip, and a penile implant to allow for erection.

Personal gender pronouns (PGPs): The pronoun or set of pronouns that a person would like others to call them by, when their proper name is not being used. Traditional examples include "she/her/hers" or "he/him/his." Some people prefer gender-neutral pronouns, such as "ze/hir/hirs," "zie/zir/zirs," or "they/them/their." Some people prefer no pronouns at all (see Bongiovanni & Jimerson, 2018).

Puberty blocking hormones: Prescribed by a physician, preferably an endocrinologist (a physician who specializes in the study of hormones or hormone-related conditions), for pre-pubertal T/GE young people to postpone the onset or completion of puberty.

Queer: Originally used with negative connotations, but is currently being reclaimed by many within the LGBTQA community. It is sometimes used as an umbrella term for many non-heterosexual identities.

Sex (anatomical/biological): Separate from gender, the physical structure of one's reproductive organs that is used to assign sex at birth. Biological sex is determined by chromosomes (XX for female, XY for males), hormones (estrogen/progesterone for females, testosterone for males), and internal and external genitalia (vulva, clitoris, vagina for females, penis and testicles for males). Given the potential variation in all of these, biological sex must be seen as a spectrum or range of possibilities rather than a binary set of two options.

Sexual minority stress: Related to societal stigma, prejudice and discrimination towards individuals with diverse gender identity and expression.

Sexual orientation: Describes sexual attraction only, and is not directly related to gender identity. The sexual orientation of T/GE people should be defined by the individual. It is often described based on the lived gender; a T/GE woman attracted to other women would be a lesbian, a T/GE woman attracted to a man would identify as heterosexual; a T/GE man attracted to other men would be a gay man, a T/GE man attracted to a woman would identify as heterosexual.

Social transition: The time when a T/GE person begins presenting in public according to their affirmed gender identity rather than according to their designated sex. Social transition refers to a number of changes that can be made in a T/GE person's social life and situation, including: use of a different name; use of different personal gender pronouns; outward transformations of the physical appearance (e.g. dressing in the chosen style, adopting a different haircut); and use of a bathroom that suits the person's affirmed gender more accurately.

They/them/their: Neutral personal gender pronouns used by some who have a non-binary or diverse gender identity.

Top surgery: Chest surgery such as double mastectomy or periareolar (keyhole) surgeries.

Trans: An umbrella term encompassing all T/GE and transsexual individuals.

Trans-affirming practice: A culturally sensitive model for working with T/GE people. This model views T/GE identity through an affirming and non-pathological lens. It is a description of practice that arises out of the context of a dominant culture in society, which attempts to regulate and specify according to normative notions of gender and sexuality. It arises out of a discourse of power that asks questions about how operations of power have been and are carried out. Trans-affirming practice encourages an idea of a constantly evolving relationship between theory and practice. It recognizes the influences on our thinking and practice of different contexts such as race, culture, class, ability, gender and sexuality.

Transgender: An umbrella term describing people whose gender identity or expression differs from that associated with their sex designated at birth.

Transition: The process by which a T/GE individual strives to have physical presentation more closely aligned with internal affirmed gender identity. Transition can occur in different ways: social transition through non-permanent changes in clothing, hairstyle, name and/or personal gender pronouns; or medical transition through the use of medicines such as hormone blockers or cross-hormones to promote gender-based body changes; and/or surgical transition in which an individual's body is modified through the addition or removal of gender-related physical traits.

Transman: A person who was designated female at birth but whose affirmed gender identity is male.

Transmasculine/transfeminine: Describe gender-diverse or non-binary persons, based on the directionality of their gender identity. A transmasculine person has a masculine spectrum gender identity, with the sex of female listed on their original birth certificate. A transfeminine person has a feminine spectrum gender identity, with the sex of male listed on their original birth certificate.

Transphobic: Negative attitudes and feelings toward T/GE individuals or discomfort with people whose gender identity and/or gender expression do not conform to traditional or stereotypic gender roles.

Transsexual: An older term for people whose gender identities don't match the sex that was designated at birth and who desire or seek to transition to bring their bodies into alignment with their gender identities. *Some people find this term offensive, others do not.* Only refer to someone as transsexual if they tell you that's how they identify.

Transwoman: A person who was designated male at birth but whose affirmed gender identity is female.

Vaginal construction/vaginoplasty: A procedure in which surgeons remove the penis and testes, if still present, and use tissues from the penis to construct the vagina, clitoris and labia.

World Professional Association for Transgender Health (WPATH): Formerly the Harry Benjamin International Gender Dysphoria Association. This is a professional organization devoted to the understanding and treatment of gender dysphoria. WPATH publishes the Standards of Care for the Health of Transsexual, Transgender, and Gender-Nonconforming People, educates professionals and consumers, sponsors scientific conferences, and provides ethical guidelines for professionals. The first version of the Standards of Care was published in 1979. Version 7 was published in 2011.

Outdated, inaccurate or offensive gender identity terms

Although some people may use the following terms to describe their own gender, most of the labels below range from out-of-date to offensive:

Gender identity disorder (GID): The preferred term is gender dysphoria.

Hermaphrodite: The preferred term is intersex.

Pre-operative, post-operative (also pre-op or post-op): Describe a T/GE person who has had or not had sex-reassignment surgeries. Focusing on whether someone has had surgery can be considered invasive or a violation of someone's privacy. Also many T/GE people don't want (or don't have access to) surgeries that will change their body. Lastly, there are a variety of other ways T/GE people transition besides sex-reassignment surgery.

Sex change operation: Preferred terms are sex-reassignment surgery (SRS) or gender-affirming surgery.

Shemale: An offensive term for a T/GE woman, especially one who has had medical treatment for her breasts, but still has a penis. This term may be used by sex workers or within the porn industry.

Tranny (sometimes referred to as the T-word): While some T/GE people use the word tranny to describe their gender, most find it highly offensive—a derogatory slur.

Transgendered: Adding -ed to the end of T/GE isn't grammatically correct. You wouldn't say that someone is gayed, womaned or Latinoed. Similarly, you wouldn't call someone transgendered.

Transgender symbols

Popular symbols used to identify the T/GE community frequently consist of modified traditional gender symbols that combine elements from both the male and female symbols.

The most common and universally accepted T/GE pride symbol depicts a circle with a cross projecting from the bottom, forming the symbol of Venus (female), an arrow projecting from the top-right, forming the symbol of Mars (male), and with an additional striked arrow (combining the female cross and male arrow) projecting from the top left. The symbol is most commonly rendered in blue with a pink triangle as its background.

Although this particular configuration of the male and female gender symbols may have been used before, the present accepted opinion is that it originated with the American Gender Talk radio station sometime before 2002. The symbol originated from a drawing by Holly Boswell of North Carolina, US. Boswell passed the design on to Wendy Pierce of the International Foundation for Gender Education (IFGE), who in turn passed it on to the founder of Gender Talk, Nancy Nangeroni, for computer generation.

Aside from the basic, standard T/GE symbols that were designed to represent "T/GE" as a gender itself, other popular, variant symbols were also designed to represent the T/GE community, as well as other specific areas of T/GE groups and/or issues. These symbols include the following:

Inverted purple triangle: This features the universal T/GE symbol set inside an inverted purple triangle, and is commonly used as a universal symbol for the T/GE community.

T/GE Pride flag: The T/GE Pride flag was created by Monica Helms in 1999, and was first flown at a Pride parade in Phoenix, Arizona in 2000. The light blue stripes signify the traditional color for baby boys, while the soft pink stripes signify the traditional color for baby girls. The white stripe signifies those who are intersex, transitioning or who identify with a neutral or undefined gender.

Transgender symbol: This symbol combines and modifies elements of the male and female gender symbols, with a symbol jutting from the top left. Denise Leclair, Executive Director of the IFGE, said the symbol was created by Nancy Nangeroni, Holly Boswell and Wendy Pierce of the IFGE.

Stonewall

The Stonewall riots, also called the Stonewall Uprising, began in the early morning of June 28, 1969 when police raided the Stonewall Inn, a gay club located in Greenwich Village in New York City. The raid sparked a riot among bar patrons and neighborhood residents, as police roughly hauled employees and patrons out of the bar. It led to six days of protests and violent clashes with law enforcement outside the bar on Christopher Street, in neighboring streets and in nearby Christopher Park.

The Stonewall riots served as a catalyst for the gay rights movement in the US and around the world. Two T/GE activists, Marsha P. Johnson and Sylvia Rivera, were among a group of people who in the 1960s stood on the front lines of the LGBT liberation movement. Johnson and Rivera, who together founded one of the first organizations (Street Transvestite Action Revolutionaries—STAR) to protect T/GE youth, were noted community workers in New York's Greenwich Village. Johnson and Rivera were part of the "vanguard" that resisted police during the Stonewall riots.

Appendix B: Transgender and Gender-Expansive Youth Resources

General information

Family Acceptance Project

https://familyproject.sfsu.edu/family-education-booklet

This Project is based at San Francisco State University and involved research and the production of a wonderful booklet focusing on the positive impact of family support for LGBTQ youth.

Gender Spectrum

www.genderspectrum.org

A support site with online forums for both teens and parents. The organization also hosts annual conferences.

Human Rights Campaign

https://www.hrc.org/resources/transgender-children-and-youth-talking-to-doctors-and-medical-providers

Advice on talking to doctors and medical providers.

It Gets Better Project

www.itgetsbetter.org

An organization that inspires youth to communicate and share their stories with the underlying message "that life does get better."

National Center for Lesbian Rights

www.Nclrights.org

An organization dedicated to advancing civil rights for all LGBTQ people and their families through advocacy and collaboration.

National Center for Transgender Equality

https://transequality.org

A national legal organization dedicated to advancing the rights of T/GE people and their families.

PFLAG

https://pflag.org

The largest family and ally organization for uniting LGBTQ family, friends and allies.

TransBucket

www.transbucket.com

A wonderful resource for those with questions about gender-affirming surgery and hormone options. It also provides a wealth of information on almost every topic that relates to anyone who is T/GE.

Transgender Advocacy Network

www.thetaskforce.org/trans-advocacy-network-launches-new-resources-for-local-organizations-to-advance-momentum-for-transgender-equality-across-the-country

An alliance of T/GE organizations that work at the state and local levels.

Transparent

www.transparentusa.org

An organization with support groups for parents with T/GE children.

Trans Youth Equality

www.transyouthequality.org

Provides education, advocacy and support for T/GE children, youth and families. It has two particularly good resources that are helpful focusing on coming out and disclosure.

Suicide prevention hotlines
Transgender Lifeline

https://translifeline.org

A suicide hotline run for and by T/GE people of all ages.

The Trevor Project

www.thetrevorproject.org

The number one LGBTQ youth suicide hotline, with excellent resources.

Legal advocacy organizations
American Civil Liberties Union

www.aclu.org

An organization that provides legal counsel and information regarding federal, state and local laws pertaining to T/GE people.

Lambda Legal

www.lambdalegal.org

An organization that focuses on litigation, education and public policy work for LGBT people.

Transgender Law and Policy Institute

www.transgenderlaw.org

An organization that focuses on law and policy issues designed to advance T/GE equality.

Youth and family conferences in the US and internationally
Black Transgender Advocacy

https://blacktrans.org

Gender Infinity, Houston

https://genderinfinity.org

Gender Odyssey, Seattle

www.genderodyssey.org

International Lesbian, Gay, Bisexual, Transgender and Intersex Association

https://ilga.org

Sparkle (UK)

www.sparkle.org.uk

Trans Tagung Muenchen (Germany)

www.transtagung-muenchen.com

True Colors LGBT Conference, Connecticut

https://ourtruecolors.org

Summer camps
Camp Aranu'tiq

www.camparanutiq.org

A camp for T/GE young people in a totally safe environment.

Rainbow Camp

www.welcomefriend.ca

A camp for LGBTQA youth, their siblings and children in queer families in the heart of Canada.

Educational resources
GLSEN

www.glsen.org

The largest national education organization to ensure safe schools for all young people.

NCTE's School Action Center

https://transequality.org/schoolaction

NCTE/GLSEN Model School District Policy

https://transequality.org/sites/default/files/images/resources/trans_school_district_model_policy_FINAL.pdf

Schools in Transition: A Guide for Supporting Transgender Students in K-12 Schools

www.hrc.org/resources/schools-in-transition-a-guide-for-supporting-transgender-students-in-k-12-s

The Department of Education's Examples of Policies and Emerging Practices for Supporting T/GE Students

www2.ed.gov/about/offices/list/oese/oshs/emergingpractices.pdf

Health care
American Academy of Pediatrics

www.aap.org

A professional membership organization of pediatricians, with excellent resources for gender identity in T/GE children.

The World Professional Association for Transgender Health (WPATH)

www.wpath.org

A professional organization devoted to the understanding and treatment of gender dysphoria with 500 members from around the world, in fields such as medicine, psychology, law, social work and counseling. This is also the site for the Standards of Care.

International organizations for T/GE people
AFRICA
South Africa

Iranti

https://www.iranti.org.za

Devex

www.devex.com/organizations/transgender-intersex-africa-111278

Gender Dynamix

www.genderdynamix.org.za

ASIA
Asia-Pacific Islanders

Asia Pacific Transgender Network

https://weareaptn.org

India

Sahodari Foundation

https://sahodari.org

Philippines

Association of Transgender People in the Philippines

www.facebook.com/philtransmov

Singapore

Oogachaga

www.oogachaga.com

Taiwan

Taiwan Tongzhi (LGBTQ+) Hotline Association

https://give2asia.org/taiwantongzhi

AUSTRALIA
Gender Centre

https://gendercentre.org.au

Transcend Support

https://transcendaus.org

EUROPE
Transgender Europe
TGEU is a member-based organization created in 2005 and a legitimate voice for
the T/GE community in Europe and Central Asia. It has 140 member organizations
in 44 different countries.

https://tgeu.org/about-us

France
Association Nationale Transgenre

https://ant-france.eu

Ireland
Transgender Equality Network Ireland

www.teni.ie

Scotland
Scottish Trans

www.scottishtrans.org

Switzerland
Transgender Network Switzerland

www.tgns.ch/fr

United Kingdom
Mermaids

https://mermaids.org.uk

LATIN AMERICA
Argentina
Asociación Travesties Transexuales y Transgeneros Argentinas

www.attta.org.ar

Brazil
The Association of Gays, Lesbians, and Transgender Persons of Santana

www.fundobrasil.org.br/projeto/aglts-associacao-de-gays-lesbicas-e-transgeneros-de-santana

Colombia
Fundación Red Comunitaria Trans

www.facebook.com/pages/category/Community/Red-Comunitaria-Trans-255992844505189

Cuba
Cuba's National Centre for Sexual Education (CENESEX)

https://www.facebook.com/cenesex

Dominican Republic
Trans Siempre Amigas (TRANSSA)

http://transsadominicana1.blogspot.com

Ecuador
Proyecto Transgenero

www.proyecto-transgenero.org

El Salvador
Asociacion Aspidh Arcoiris Trans

www.facebook.com/AspidhArcoirisTrans

Guatemala
Red Multicultural de Mujeres Trans de Guatemala (REDMMUTRANS)

www.facebook.com/redmmutrans.guatemala

Haiti
Transgender Haiti

www.facebook.com/pages/category/Nonprofit-Organization/Transgender-Haiti-1972059669511237

Nicaragua
Organization of Transgender People of Nicaragua (ODETRANS)

www.facebook.com/odetrans/posts_to_page

Peru
Unicxs

www.unicxs.org/unicxse

Sample policies

Best Practices for Non-Binary Inclusion in the Workplace: http://outandequal.org/app/uploads/2018/11/OE-Non-Binary-Best-Practices.pdf

Model District Policy on Transgender and Nonconforming Students: https://www.glsen.org/activity/model-local-education-agency-policy-on-transgender-nonbinary-students

Model Restroom Access Policies: www.lambdalegal.org/know-your-rights/article/trans-model-restroom-policies

Model Transgender Employment Policy: https://transgenderlawcenter.org/wp-content/uploads/2013/12/model-workplace-employment-policy-Updated.pdf

Model Transgender Shelter Policy: https://transgenderlawcenter.org/wp-content/uploads/2016/01/12.30.2015-Model-Homeless-Shelter-TG-Policy.pdf

Transitioning Our Shelters: A Guide to Making Homeless Shelters Safe for Transgender People: https://srlp.org/wp-content/uploads/2012/08/TransitioningOurShelters.pdf

Workplace Gender Identity and Transition Guidelines: http://outandequal.org/app/uploads/2016/09/Transition-Guidelines-Full-Edition.pdf

Books for parents of T/GE young people

Becoming Nicole: The Transformation of an American Family, Amy Ellis Nutt (2015). The inspiring story of identical twins, one of whom is T/GE, and the journey to acceptance.

Being Jazz: My Life as a (Transgender) Teen, Jazz Jennings (2016). The story of a T/GE child based on the real-life experience of Jazz Jennings, who has become a spokesperson for T/GE kids everywhere.

The Bold World: A Memoir of Family and Transformation, Jodie Patterson (2019). The narrative of an African American mother reshaping her attitudes and beliefs, as well as those of her community, to meet the needs of her T/GE son and opening the minds of everyone in her family.

Felix Ever After, Kacen Callender (2020). When Felix has his dead name and pre-transition photos publicly outed, he seeks revenge. He questions whether identifying as a T/GE boy is 100 percent the right label for him when he doesn't feel like a boy *all* the time. A story about self-discovery and personal passions, the complexity of human relationships and being multiply marginalized.

Gender Born, Gender Made: Raising Health Gender-Nonconforming Children, Diane Ehrensaft (2011). Offers parents, clinicians and educators guidance on both the ethical dilemmas and the practical, daily concerns of working with children who don't fit a "typical" gender mold. She provides new insights into the outmoded approaches to gender nonconformity that may actually harm children. Ehrensaft presents a new framework for helping each child become his or her own unique, most gender-authentic person.

The Gender Identity Workbook for Kids, Kelly Storck (2018). A comprehensive workbook with clearly explained concepts, and with a sensitivity, insight, caring and compassion, written for parents and professionals. It offers fun, age-appropriate activities to help children explore their identity and discover unique ways to navigate gender expression at home, in school and with friends. This is a valuable resource to go back to frequently on the gender journey of self-discovery, deeply affirming of the uniqueness and worth of every person.

I am J, Cris Beam (2011). An engaging novel about J, a young Latinx T/GE boy coming of age, coming out, and beginning to transition while in high school. The book touches on familiar issues such as struggles in school, romance, and the challenges of relating to family members and friends during a time of self-discovery. Ultimately, however, Beam's work is a story of resilience and J's path to knowing self-love, finding support and standing up for himself.

The Last Time I Wore a Dress, Daphne Scholinski (1998). This brilliant memoir recounts the author's life as a girl who liked to ride her bike without a shirt and the drama that it caused when she did that. It also recalls the three years spent in psychiatric hospitals for, among other things, gender dysphoria (called gender identity disorder at the time). Because they were a tomboy who wore jeans and T-shirts and didn't act enough like a girl, their treatment, in addition to talk therapy, isolation and drugs, required them to wear make-up and walk "like a girl."

Nonbinary: Memoirs of Gender and Identity, Micah Rajunov and Scott Duane (eds) (2019). First-person narratives show us a world where gender exists along a spectrum, a web, a multidimensional space. Nuanced storytellers break away from mainstream portrayals of gender diversity, cutting across lines of age, race, ethnicity, ability, class, religion, family and relationships.

A Quick & Easy Guide to They/Them Pronouns, Archie Bongiovanni and Tristan Jimerson (2018). A hip genderqueer artist and a cisgender guy who produced a comic guide that explains what personal gender pronouns are, why they matter, and how to use them. They also include what to do if you make a mistake. Also see *A Quick & Easy Guide to Queer & Trans Identities* by G. Mady and J.R. Zuckerberg (2019).

Raising My Rainbow: Adventures in Raising a Fabulous, Gender Creative Son, Lori Duron (2014). A frank, heartfelt and brutally funny account of Lori and her family's adventures of distress and happiness raising a gender-creative son. Based on Lori's popular blog.

Raising Ryland: Our Story of Parenting a Transgender Child with No Strings Attached, Hillary Whittington (2016). This powerful, moving story is a mother's first-hand account of her emotional choice to embrace her T/GE child, Ryland.

Sissy: A Coming-of-Gender Story, Jacob Tobia (2019). A memoir about what it's like to grow up not sure if you're a boy, a girl, or something in between. Written with the powerful honesty, irreverent humor and authentic vulnerability that has made this a media sensation.

Stone Butch Blues, Leslie Feinberg (1993). This brilliant, original novel is one of the finest accounts ever written of the complexities of a T/GE existence.

The Transgender Generation: How Transgender Kids (and Their Parents) are Creating a Gender Revolution, Ann Travers (2019). Based on interviews with T/GE kids, ranging in age from 4 to 20, and their parents, and over five years of research in the US and Canada. First-person narratives reveal what it is like to grow up as a T/GE child.

What We Will Become: A Mother, a Son, and a Journey of Transformation, Mimi Lemay (2019). A mother's memoir of her T/GE child's odyssey, and her journey outside the boundaries of the faith and culture that shaped her.

Books for professionals

A Clinician's Guide to Gender-Affirming Care: Working with Transgender and Gender Nonconforming Clients, Sand Chang, Anneliese Singh and lore dickey (2018). An excellent resource for clinicians working with T/GE and gender-variant clients.

The Gender Creative Child: Pathways for Nurturing and Supporting Children Who Live Outside Gender Boxes, Diane Ehrensaft and Norman Spack (2016). A comprehensive resource that explains the interconnected effects of biology, nurture and culture. A guide through the rapidly changing cultural, medical and legal landscape of gender and identity.

Helping Your Transgender Teen: A Guide for Parents, Irwin Krieger (2011). A clear and concise book for the parents of T/GE teens, to help parents understand what their child is feeling and experiencing. Krieger is a clinical social worker with many years of experience helping T/GE teens.

Social Work Practice with Transgender and Gender Variant Youth, Gerald P. Mallon (ed.) (2009). Through personal narratives and case studies, this second edition explores the childhood and adolescent experiences of T/GE and gender-variant persons. The book offers suggestions that will help social workers and the youths' families learn more about the reality of T/GE persons' lives.

Supporting Transgender and Gender Creative Youth: Schools, Families, and Communities in Action, Elizabeth Meyer and Annie Pullen Sansfaçon (eds) (2014). Addresses issues and challenges in the interdisciplinary fields of education, social work, medicine and counseling. It also includes practical recommendations for parents, families, practitioners and educators.

Transgender 101: A Simple Guide to a Complex Issue, Nicholas Teich (2012). Written by a social worker and member of the T/GE community, this resource combines an accessible portrait of T/GE identity with a rich history of T/GE life and its unique experiences of discrimination.

The Transgender Child: A Handbook for Families and Professionals, Stephanie A. Brill and Rachel Pepper (2008). A comprehensive guidebook on gender expansiveness from birth through college. How can parents advocate for their children in elementary schools? What do doctors and therapists recommend?

Transgender Emergence: Therapeutic Guidelines for Working with Gender Variant People and their Families, Arlene Istar Lev (2004). This comprehensive book provides readers with a clinical and theoretical overview of the issues facing T/GE people and their families.

Transgender Kids: Pride, Joy, and Families in Transition, Elijah C. Nealy (2019). A wonderfully comprehensive guide to the medical, emotional and social issues of T/GE kids. It covers topics from family life to school and mental health issues, as well as the physical, social and emotional aspects of transition.

The Transgender Teen, Stephanie A. Brill and Lisa Kenney (2016). This comprehensive guidebook explores the unique challenges that thousands of families face every day raising a teenager who may be T/GE, non-binary, gender fluid or otherwise gender expansive. Combining years of practice wisdom with extensive research and personal interviews, the authors cover the major concerns relating to physical and emotional development, social and school pressures, medical considerations and family communications.

T/GE-themed films

Beautiful Boxer is a 2004 Thai film that depicts the true story of the public transition of a Thai boxer, by director Ekachai Uekrongtham. It tells the life story of Parinya Charoenphol, a famous kathoey (T/GE woman) who is a fighter, actress and model.

Boy Meets Girl—Love Transcends Gender, a 2014 film directed by Eric Schaeffer, is a sex-positive movie about growing up T/GE in a small town. T/GE actor Michelle Hendley gives a compelling performance.

Boys Don't Cry is a 1999 film, directed by Kimberly Peirce, which brutally depicts the corporeal reality of T/GE men in the rural US. Following the true story of T/GE man Brandon Teena, portrayed by cis woman actor Hilary Swank, the film documents one of the most well-known murders of a T/GE person in Humboldt, Nebraska in December 1993 at the hands of men driven by prejudice and hatred after they discovered that he was trans. Teena's life, and ultimate death, is a love story. Away from home, Teena pursues a life as himself, without sharing his gendered past with the woman he falls in love with, or her friends and family—a group of deeply bigoted, backwoods white men.

A Fantastic Woman is a 2017 Chilean drama directed by Sebastián Lelio which tells the story of Marina, a young T/GE woman living in Santiago, who has to navigate the transphobia she encounters after the death of her boyfriend. Marina is beautifully played by T/GE actress Daniela Vega, who perfectly portrays the distress but also her pride and defiance.

Hedwig and the Angry Inch is a 2001 musical comedy-drama film directed by John Cameron Mitchell. It chronicles the life and career of Hedwig Robinson, a T/GE East German singer of a fictional rock band.

Ma Vie en Rose (English translation: *My Life in Pink*) is a 1997 Belgian film directed by Alain Berliner. It beautifully tells the story of Ludovic, a child who is seen by family and community as a boy, but consistently communicates that he is a girl-boy. Few viewers could be left unmoved by the scene where Ludo's hair is forcibly cut—the simplicity of gender markers for children, and their importance, is what makes this film so affecting. Ultimately, the film depicts Ludovic's family's struggle to accept and deal with their emerging gender expression.

Paris is Burning is a 1990 film, directed by Jennie Livingston. This classic film highlights the narratives of young African American and Latino people of various gender identities who competed in New York's glamorous balls. It explores race, class, sexuality and gender with intelligence, sensitivity and humor. It follows several real-life young people who walked down a runway, being judged on the "realness" in the ballroom scene of New York City in the 1980s (Arnold & Bailey, 2009). The film is about how communities are formed by these young people who had finally found a place where their difference was celebrated rather than scorned. The young people speak candidly about facing racism, homophobia, transphobia, poverty and the AIDS crisis, being thrown out of their homes, shoplifting or becoming sex workers as they struggle to survive in a hostile world.

Pose is an American drama television series about New York City's African American and Latino LGBTQ and gender-expansive ballroom culture scene in the 1980s and, in the second season, the early 1990s (Murphy, Falchuk & Canals, 2018). Featured characters are dancers and models who compete for trophies and recognition in the ballroom scene, and who support one another in a network of chosen families known as Houses.

Southern Comfort is a 2001 documentary film, directed by Mark Patrick George and focusing on the final year in the life of Robert Eads, a T/GE man. Eads, diagnosed with ovarian cancer, was turned down for treatment by a dozen doctors out of fear that treating such a patient would hurt their reputations. By the time Eads received treatment, the cancer was too advanced to save his life.

Tomboy is a 2011 French drama film written and directed by Céline Sciamma. The story follows a ten-year-old gender-variant child, Laure, who moves to a new neighborhood during the summer holiday and experiments with their gender presentation, adopting the name Mikäel.

References

Able-Peterson, T. & Bucy, J. (1993). *The Street Outreach Training Manual*. Washington, DC: US Department of Health and Human Services.

Abramovich, A. (2016). Understanding how policy and culture create oppressive conditions for LGBTQ2S youth in the shelter system. *Journal of Homosexuality, 64*(11), 1484–1501.

Abramovich, A. & Shelton, J.E. (2017). *Where am I Going to Go? Intersectional Approaches to Ending LGBTQ2S Youth Homelessness in Canada & the U.S.* Toronto, ON: Canadian Observatory on Homelessness Press.

Allen, B.J., Andert, B., Botsford, J., Budge, S.L. & Rehm, J.L. (2020). At the margins: Comparing school experiences of nonbinary and binary-identified transgender youth. *Journal of School Health, 25*, 2231–2331.

American Psychological Association. (2013). *Diagnostic and Statistical Manual of Mental Disorders* (fifth edition). Washington, DC: Author.

American Public Health Association. (2016). Promoting transgender and gender minority health through inclusive policies and practices (Policy No. 20169). Retrieved from www.apha.org/policies-and-advocacy/public-health-policy-statements/policy-database/2017/01/26/promoting-transgender-and-gender-minority-health-through-inclusive-policies-and-practices.

Ansara, Y.G. & Hegarty, P. (2012). Cisgenderism in psychology: Pathologizing and misgendering children from 1999 to 2008. *Psychology & Sexuality, 3*, 137–160.

Aramburu Alegría, C. (2018). Supporting families of transgender children/youth: Parents speak on their experiences, identity, and views. *International Journal of Transgenderism, 19*(2), 132–143.

Arnold, E. & Bailey, M. (2009). Constructing home and family: How the ballroom community supports African American GLBTQ youth in the face of HIV/AIDS. *Journal of Gay & Lesbian Social Services, 21*(2/3), 171–188.

Asscheman, H., Giltay, E.J., Megens, J.A.J., de Ronde, W., van Trotsenburg, M.A.A. & Gooren, L.J.G. (2011). A long-term follow-up study of mortality in transsexuals receiving treatment with cross-sex hormones. *European Journal of Endocrinology, 164*(4), 635–642.

Bauer, G., Hammond, R., Travers, R., Kaay, M., Hohenadel, K. & Boyce, M. (2009). "I don't think this is theoretical; this is our lives": How erasure impacts health care for transgender people. *Journal of the Association of Nurses in AIDS Care, 20*(5), 348–361.

Becerra-Culqui, T.A., Liu, Y., Nash, R. Cromwell, L., *et al.* (2018). Mental health of transgender and gender nonconforming youth compared with their peers. *Journal of Pediatrics, 141*(5), e20173845.

Begun, S. & Kattari, S.K. (2015). Conforming for survival: Associations between transgender visual conformity/passing and homelessness experiences. *Journal of Gay & Lesbian Social Services, 28*(1), 54–66.

Berliner, A. (director, co-writer) & Scotta, C. (producer) (1997). *Ma Vie en Rose* [film]. Available from SONY Classics, Los Angeles.

Birnkrant, J.M. & Przeworski, A. (2017). Communication, advocacy, and acceptance among support-seeking parents of transgender youth. *Journal of Gay & Lesbian Mental Health, 21*(2), 132–153.

Blair, K. & Hoskin, R. (2018). Transgender exclusion from the world of dating: Patterns of acceptance and rejection of hypothetical T/GE dating partners as a function of sexual and gender identity. *Journal of Social and Personal Relationships, 36*(7), 2074–2095.

Bockting, W.O. (2013). Transgender Identity Development. In D.L. Tolman & L.M. Diamond (eds), *APA Handbook of Sexuality and Psychology: Vol 1 Person-Based Approaches* (pp.739–758). Washington, DC: American Psychological Association.

Bockting, W.O., Miner, M.H., Swinburne, R., Rebecca, E., Hamilton, A. & Coleman, E. (2013). Stigma, mental health, and resilience in an online sample of the US transgender population. *American Journal of Public Health, 103*(5), 943–951.

Boivin, L., Notredame, C., Jardri, R., Medjkane, F. *et al.* (2020). Supporting parents of transgender adolescents: Yes, but how? *Archives of Sexual Behavior, 49*, 81–83.

Bongiovanni, A. & Jimerson, T. (2018). *A Quick and Easy Guide to They/Them Pronouns*. Portland, OR: Limerance Press.

Brill, S. & Kenney, L. (2016). *The Transgender Teen: A Handbook for Parents and Professionals Supporting Transgender and Non-Binary Teens*. Jersey City, NJ: Cleis Press.

Brill, S. & Pepper, R. (2008). *The Transgender Child: A Handbook for Families and Professionals*. Jersey City, NJ: Cleis Press.

Brown, T.N.T., Herman, J.L. & Park, A.S. (2017). *Exploring International Priorities and Best Practices for the Collection of Data about Gender Minorities, Report of Meeting*. Los Angeles, CA: The Williams Institute.

Bullard, L., Owens, L.W., Richmond, L. & Alwon, F. (eds). (2010). Residential issues in child welfare. *Child Welfare, 89*(2).

Burgess, C. (2009). Internal and External Stress Factors Associated with the Identity Development of Transgender Youth. In G.P. Mallon (ed.), *Social Work Practice with Transgender and Gender Variant Youth* (second edition) (pp.35–48). New York, NY: Routledge.

Butler, J. (1999). *Gender Trouble: Feminism and the Subversion of Identity*. New York, NY: Routledge.

Chan, C.D. (2018). Families as transformative allies to transgender youth of color: Positioning intersectionality as analysis to demarginalize political systems of oppression. *Journal of GLBT Family Studies, 14*(1–2), 43–60.

Chang, S.C., Singh, A.A. & dickey, l.m. (2018). *A Clinician's Guide to Gender-Affirming Care: Working with Transgender and Gender Nonconforming Clients*. Oakland, CA: Context Press.

Charles, R. (writer). (2018). *RuPaul's Drag Race* [television series]. RuPaul Charles (executive producer). New York, NY: World of Wonder Productions.

Clark, B.A., Marshall, S.K. & Saewyc, E.M. (2020). Hormone therapy decision-making processes: Transgender youth and parents. *Journal of Adolescence, 79*, 136–147.

Clements, J.A. & Rosenwald, M. (2007). Foster parents' perspectives on LGB youth in the child welfare system. *Journal of Gay & Lesbian Social Services: Issues in Practice, Policy & Research, 19*(1), 57–69.

Coleman, E., Bockting, W., Botzer, M., Cohen-Kettenis, P. *et al.* (2011). Standards of care for the health of transsexual, transgender, and gender-nonconforming people, version 7. *International Journal of Transgenderism, 13*, 165–232.

Coleman, E., Bockting, W., Botzer, M., Cohen-Kettenis, P. *et al.* (2012). *Standards of Care for the Health of Transsexual, Transgender, and Gender Variant People* (seventh edition). East Dundee, IL: Author.

Cray, A., Miller, K. & Durso, L.E. (2013). *Seeking Shelter: The Experiences and Unmet Needs of LGBT Homeless Youth*. Washington, DC: Center for American Progress.

Cruz, T.M. (2014). Assessing access to care for transgender and gender nonconforming people: A consideration of diversity in combating discrimination. *Social Science & Medicine, 110*, 65–73.

Currah, P., Juang, R.M. & Minter, S.P. (eds). (2006). *Transgender Rights*. Minneapolis, MN: University of Minnesota Press.

Davis, C. (2008). Social Work with Transgender and Gender Variant Persons. In G.P. Mallon (ed.), *Social Work Practice with Lesbian, Gay, Bisexual, and Transgender People* (pp.212–242). New York, NY: Routledge.

DeCrescenzo, T. & Mallon, G.P. (2000). *Serving Transgender Youth: The Role of Child Welfare Systems*. Washington, DC: CWLA Press.

Deutsch, M.B. (2016). *Guidelines for the Primary and Gender-Affirming Care of Transgender and Gender Nonbinary People* (second edition). San Francisco, CA: The Center of Excellence for Transgender Health at the University of California, San Francisco.

Devor, A.H. (2004). Witnessing and mirroring: A fourteen stage model of transsexual identity formation. *Journal of Gay and Lesbian Psychotherapy, 8*, 41–67.

De Vries, A.L.C., Cohen-Kettenis, P.T. & Delemarre-Van de Waal, H. (2006). Clinical Management of Gender Dysphoria in Adolescents. In *Caring for Transgender Adolescents in BC: Suggested Guidelines.* Vancouver, British Columbia, Canada: Transgender Health Program.

De Vries, A.L.C., McGuire, J.K., Steensma, T.D., Wagenaar, E.C.F., Doreleijers, T.A.H. & Cohen-Kettenis, P. (2014). Young adult psychological outcome after puberty suppression and gender reassignment. *Pediatrics, 134*(4), 696–704.

Diamond, L. (2008). *Sexual Fluidity: Understanding Women's Love and Desire.* Cambridge, MA: Harvard University Press.

Drescher, J. & Pula, J. (2014). Ethical issues raised by the treatment of gender-variant prepubescent children. LGBT bioethics: Visibility, disparities and dialogue. *Hastings Center Report, 44*(5), S17–S22.

Edwards-Leeper, L., Leibowitz, S. & Sangganjanavanich, V.F. (2016). Affirmative practice transgender and gender nonconforming youth: Expanding the model. *Psychology of Sexual Orientation and Gender Diversity, 3*(2), 165–172.

Ehrensaft, D. (2011). *Gender Born, Gender Made: Raising Health Gender Variant Children.* New York, NY: The Experiment.

Ehrensaft, D. (2012). From gender identity disorder to gender identity creativity: True gender self child therapy. *Journal of Homosexuality, 59*(3), 337–356.

Ehrensaft, D. (2014). Found in transition: Our littlest transgender people. *Contemporary Psychoanalysis, 50*(4), 571–592.

Ehrensaft, D. (2016). *The Gender Creative Child: Pathways for Nurturing and Supporting Children Who Live Outside Gender Boxes.* New York, NY: The Experiment.

Elze, D. & McHaelen, R. (2009). *Moving the Margins: Training Curriculum for Child Welfare Services with Lesbian, Gay, Bisexual, Transgender, and Questioning (LGBTQ) Youth in Out-of-Home Care: Train the Trainer Manual.* Washington, DC: National Association of Social Workers.

Fernandes-Alcantara, A.L. (2018). *Runaway and Homeless Youth: Demographics and Programs*. Washington, DC: Congressional Research Service.

Fox, M.M. (2019). Why you should consider transgender awareness training in your workplace. *Forbes,* 113–117.

Freeman, L. & Hamilton, D. (2008*). A Count of Homeless Youth in New York City*. New York, NY: Empire State Coalition of Youth and Family Services.

Frohard-Dourlent, H., Dobson, S., Clark, B.A., Doull, M. & Saewyc, E.M. (2017). "I would have preferred more options": Accounting for non-binary youth in health research. *Nursing Inquiry, 24*(1), 1–9.

Gallegos, A., White, C., Ryan, C., O'Brien, K., Pecora, P. & Thomas, P. (2011). Exploring the experiences of lesbian, gay, bisexual, and questioning adolescents in foster care. *Journal of Family Social Work, 14,* 226–236.

Glenn, W. (2009). "For Colored Girls": Reflections of an Emerging Male to Female Transgender and Gender Variant Youth Consciousness. In G.P. Mallon (ed.), *Social Work Practice with Transgender and Gender Variant Youth* (second edition) (pp.83–94). New York, NY: Routledge.

Goffman, E. (1963). *Stigma: Notes on the Management of Spoiled Identity*. Englewood Cliffs, NJ: Prentice-Hall.

Gonzalez, K. (2019). *Trans+: Love, Sex, Romance, and Being You*. Washington, DC: Magination Press.

Gower, A.L., Rider, G.N., Brown, C., McMorris, B.J. *et al.* (2018). Supporting transgender and gender diverse youth: Protection against emotional distress and substance use. *American Journal of Preventive Medicine, 55*(6), 787–794.

Grant, J.M., Mottet, L.A., Tanis, J., Harrison, J., Herman, J.L. & Keisling, M. (2011). *Injustice at Every Turn: A Report of the National Transgender Discrimination Survey*. Washington, DC: National Center for Transgender Equality and National Gay and Lesbian Task Force.

Gray, S.A., Sweeney, K.K., Randazzo, R. & Levitt, H.M. (2016). "Am I doing the right thing?": Pathways to parenting a gender variant child. *Family Process, 55*(1), 123–138.

Green, J. (2017). Legal issues for transgender people: A review of persistent threats. *Sexual Health, 14*(5), 431–435.

Gridley, S.J., Crouch, J.M., Evans, Y., Eng, W. *et al.* (2016). Youth and caregiver perspectives on barriers to gender-affirming health care for transgender youth. *Journal of Adolescent Health, 59*(3), 254–261.

Grossman, A.H. & D'Augelli, A.R. (2006). Transgender youth: Invisible and vulnerable. *Journal of Homosexuality, 51*(1), 111–128.

Grossman, A.H. & D'Augelli., A.R. (2007). Transgender youth and life-threatening behaviors. *Suicide and Life-Threatening Behaviors, 37*(5), 527–537.

Grossman, A.H., D'Augelli, A.R., Howell, T.J. & Hubbard, S. (2006a). Parental reactions to transgender youth's gender variant expression and identity. *Journal of Gay & Lesbian Social Services, 18*(1), 3–16.

Grossman, A.H., D'Augelli, A.R. & Salter, N.P. (2006b). Male to female transgender youth: Gender expression milestones, gender atypicality, victimization, and parents' responses. *Journal of GLBT Family Studies, 2*(1), 71–92.

Haas, A., Rodgers, P. & Herman, J. (2017). *Suicide Attempts Among Transgender and Gender Variant Adults*. Los Angeles, CA: The Williams Institute.

Hatchel, T. & Marx, R. (2018). Understanding intersectionality and resiliency among transgender adolescents: Exploring pathways among peer victimization, school belonging, and drug use. *International Journal of Environmental Research and Public Health, 15,* 1289.

Hembree, W.C., Cohen-Kettenis, P.T., Gooren, L., Hannema, S.E. *et al.* (2017). Endocrine treatment of gender-dysphoric/gender-incongruent persons: An Endocrine Society clinical practice guideline. *The Journal of Clinical Endocrinology & Metabolism, 102*(11), 3869–3903.

Herman, J. (2013). Gendered restrooms and minority stress: The public regulation of gender and its impact on transgender people's lives. *Journal of Public Management and Social Policy, 19*(1), 65–80.

Hill, D.B. & Menvielle, E. (2009). "You have to give them a place where they feel protected and safe and loved": The views of parents who have gender-variant children and adolescents. *Journal of LGBT Youth, 6*(2–3), 243–271.

Hill, D.B., Menvielle, E., Sica, K. & Johnson, A. (2010). An affirming intervention for families with gender variant children: Parental ratings of child mental health and gender. *Journal of Sex and Marital Therapy, 36*(1), 6–23.

Human Rights Campaign (HRC). (2019). *Transgender inclusion in the workplace: Recommended policies and practices.* Washington, DC: Author.

Human Rights Campaign. (2020). *Inclusive interpretation of the sex discrimination law.* Washington, DC: Author.

Iantaffi, A. & Bockting, W.O. (2011). Views from both sides of the bridge? Gender, sexual legitimacy and transgender people's experiences of relationships. *Culture, Health and Sexuality, 13*, 355–370.

Irvine, A. (2010). "We've Had Three of Them": Addressing the invisibility of lesbian, gay, bisexual, and gender nonconforming youths in the juvenile justice system. *Columbia Journal of Gender and Law, 19*(3), 675–701.

Irvine, A. & Canfield, A. (2015). The overrepresentation of lesbian, gay, bisexual, questioning, gender nonconforming and transgender youth within the child welfare to juvenile justice crossover population. *Journal of Gender, Social Policy, & the Law, 24*(2), 243–261.

Israel, G. & Tarver, D. (1998). *Transgender Care: Recommended Guidelines, Practical Information and Personal Accounts.* Philadelphia: Temple University Press.

James, A., Miller, C.K. & St. John, D. (executive producers) (2018). *I am Jazz.* Coral Springs, FL: This is Just a Test.

James, S.E., Herman, J.L., Rankin, S., Keisling, M., Mottet, L. & Anafi, M. (2016). *The Report of the 2015 U.S. Transgender Survey.* Washington, DC: National Center for Transgender Equality.

Janssen, A. & Leibowitz, S. (2018). *Affirmative Mental Health Care for Transgender and Gender Diverse Youth: A Clinical Guide.* New York, NY: Springer.

Jennings, J. (2016). *Being Jazz: My Life as a (Transgender) Teen.* New York, NY: Ember.

Johnson, T.W. & Wassersug, R.J. (2016). Recognition of gender variants outside the binary in WPATH Standards of Care, Version 7.0. *International Journal of Transgenderism, 17*(1), 1–3.

Kattari, S. & Begun, S. (2017). On the margins of the marginalized: Transgender homelessness and survival sex. *Affilia: Journal of Women and Social Work, 32*(1), 92–103.

Katz-Wise, S.L., Budge, S.L., Fugate, E., Flanagan, K. *et al.* (2017). Transactional pathways of transgender identity development in transgender and gender nonconforming youth and caregivers from the transgender youth family study. *The International Journal of Transgenderism, 18*(3), 243–263.

Koken, J.A., Bimbi, D.S. & Parsons, J.T. (2009). Experiences of familial acceptance-rejection among transwomen of color. *Journal of Family Psychology, 23*(6), 853–860.

Kosciw, J.G., Greytak, E.A., Zongrone, A.D., Clark, C.M. & Truong, N.L. (2018). *The 2017 National School Climate Survey: The Experiences of Lesbian, Gay, Bisexual, Transgender, and Queer Youth in Our Nation's Schools*. New York, NY: GLSEN.

Krieger, l. (2017). *Counseling Transgender and Non-Binary Youth: The Essential Guide*. London: Jessica Kingsley Publishers.

Kuvalanka, K., Weiner, J. & Mahan, D. (2014). Child, family, and community transformations: Findings from interviews with mothers of transgender children. *Journal of GLBT Family Therapy, 10*(4), 354–379.

Langford, J. (2018). *The Pride Guide: A Guide for Sexual and Social Health for LGBTQ Youth*. Lanham, MD: Rowman & Littlefield.

Lev, A.l. (2004). *Transgender Emergence: Therapeutic Guidelines for Working with Gender-Variant People and their Families*. New York, NY: Haworth Press.

Levin, D. (2020, March 12). A clash across America over transgender rights. *The New York Times*, p.B12. Retrieved from https://www.nytimes.com/2020/03/12/us/transgender-youth-legislation.html.

Levine, S.B. (2019). Informed consent for transgender patients. *Journal of Sex and Marital Therapy, 45*(3), 218–229.

Levitt, H.M. (2019). A psychosocial genealogy of LGBTQ+ gender: An empirically based theory of gender and gender identity cultures. *Psychology of Women Quarterly, 43*(3), 275–297.

Levitt, H.M. & lppolito, M.R. (2014). Being transgender: The experience of transgender identity development. *Journal of Homosexuality, 61*, 1727–1758.

Liptak, A. (2020, June 16). Civil rights law protects gay and transgender workers, Supreme Court rules. *The New York Times*, p.A2.

Livingston, J. (director) (1990). *Paris is Burning* [film]. Off White Productions.

Maccio, E. & Ferguson, K. (2016). Services to LGBTQ runaway and homeless youth: Gaps and recommendations. *Children and Youth Services Review, 63*, 47–57.

Mallon, G.P. (1998). *We Don't Exactly Get the Welcome Wagon: The Experience of Gay and Lesbian Adolescents in Child Welfare Systems*. New York, NY: Columbia University Press.

Mallon, G.P. (ed.). (2009). *Social Work Practice with Transgender and Gender Variant Youth* (second edition). New York, NY: Routledge.

Mallon, G.P. (ed.). (2017). *Social Work Practice with Lesbian, Gay, Bisexual, and Transgender People* (third edition). New York, NY: Routledge.

Mallon, G.P. & DeCrescenzo, T. (2017). Social Work Practice with Transgender and Gender Variant Children and Youth. ln G.P. Mallon (ed.), *Social Work Practice with Transgender and Gender Variant Youth* (second edition) (pp.65–86). New York, NY: Routledge.

Mallon, G.P. & Perez, J. (2020). The experiences of transgender and gender expansive youth in juvenile justice systems. *Journal of Criminological Research, Policy and Practice, 6*(3), 217–229.

Marksamer, J. (2011). *A Place of Respect: A Guide for Group Care Facilities Serving Transgender and Gender Variant Youth*. San Francisco, CA: National Center for Lesbian Rights.

McCormick, A., Scheyd, K. & Terrazas, S. (2017). Policy Essay. Fostering the acceptance and inclusion of LGBTQ youth in the child welfare system: Considerations for advancing trauma informed responses for LGBTQ youth in care. *Journal of Family Strengths, 17*(2), 21–26.

McGuire, J. & Conover-Williams, M. (2010). Creating spaces to support transgender youth. *The Prevention Researcher, 17*(4), 17-20.

Morton, M. (2020). The complex predictors of youth homelessness. *Journal of Adolescent Health, 66*(4), 381-382.

Morton, M., Dworsky, A., Patel, S. & Samuels, G. (2018). *LGBTQ Young Adults Experience Homelessness at More than Twice the Rate of Peers.* Chicago, IL: Chapin Hall.

Mottet, L. & Ohle, J. (2006). Transitioning our shelters: Making homeless shelters safe for transgender people. *Journal of Poverty, 10*(2), 77-101.

Movement Advancement Project. (2020). Equality maps: Identity document laws and policies. Retrieved from www.lgbtmap.org/equality-maps/identity_document_laws.

Murphy, R., Falchuk, B. & Canals, S. (writers). (2018). *Pose* [television series]. Ryan Murphy (executive producer). New York, NY: FX Productions.

Nahata, L., Quinn, G.P., Caltabellotta, N.M. & Tishelman, A.C. (2017). Mental health concerns and insurance denials among transgender adolescents. *LGBT Health, 4*(3), 188-193.

Nealy, E.C. (2019). *Trans Kids and Teens: Cultivating Pride and Joy with Families in Transition.* New York, NY: W.W. Norton.

Newcomb, M.E., Feinstein, B.A. & Matsion, M. (2018). "I have no idea what's going on out there": Parents' perspectives on promoting sexual health in lesbian, gay, bisexual, and transgender adolescents. *Sexuality Research and Social Policy, 15,* 111-122.

Newcomb, M.E., Hill, R., Buehler, K. Ryan, D.T. *et al.* (2020). High burden of mental health problems, substance use, violence, and related psychosocial factors in transgender, non-binary, and gender diverse youth and young adults. *Archives of Sexual Behavior, 49,* 645-659.

Norwood, K. (2013). Grieving gender: Trans-identities, transition, and ambiguous loss. *Communication Monographs, 80*(1), 24-45.

Olivet, J. & Dones, M. (2016). Intersectionality and Race: How Racism and Discrimination Contribute to Homelessness Among LGBTQ Youth. In C. Price, C. Wheeler, J. Shelton & M. Maury (eds), *At the Intersections: A Collaborative Report on LGBTQ Youth Homelessness.* New York, NY: True Colors Fund and the National LGBTQ Task Force.

Olson, K.R., Durwood, L., DeMeules, M. & McLaughlin, K.A. (2016). Mental health of transgender children who are supported in their identities. *Pediatrics, 137*(3), 201-210.

Orr, A., Baum, J., Brown, J., Gill, E., Kahn, E. & Salem, A. (2015). *Schools in Transition: A Guide for Supporting Transgender Students in K-12 Schools.* Washington, DC: Human Rights Campaign.

Paul, J. (2018). Under the radar: Exploring support for lesbian, gay, bisexual, transgender, queer and questioning (LGBTQ) young people transitioning from foster care to emerging adulthood. Doctoral dissertation. University of Wisconsin-Madison. Madison, WI.

Pyne, J. (2011). Unsuitable bodies: Transgender people and cisnormativity in shelter services. *Canadian Social Work Journal, 28*(1), 129-138.

Rood, B.A., Reisner, S.L., Surace, F.I., Puckett, J.A., Maroney, M.R. & Pantalone, D.W. (2016). Expecting rejection: Understanding minority stress experiences of transgender and gender-variant individuals. *Transgender Health, 1*(1), 151-164.

Ruggs, E.N., Martinez, L.R., Hebl, M.R. & Law, C.L. (2015). Workplace "trans"-actions: How organizations, coworkers, and individual openness influence perceived gender identity discrimination. *Psychology of Sexual Orientation and Gender Diversity, 2*(4), 404-412.

Russell, S. (2010). Zero tolerance and alternative discipline strategies. National Association of School Psychologists. Retrieved from www.nasponline.org/resources/ hand outs/Zero_Tolerance_35-1_S4-35.pdf.

Russell, S.T., Pollitt, A.M., Li, G. & Grossman, A.H. (2018). Chosen name use is linked to reduced depressive symptoms, suicidal ideation, and suicidal behavior among transgender youth. *Journal of Adolescent Health, 63*(4), 503–505.

Ryan, C., Huebner, D., Diaz, R.M. & Sanchez, J. (2009). Family rejection as a predictor of negative health outcomes in white and Latino lesbian, gay and bisexual young adults. *Pediatrics, 123*, 346–352.

Ryan, C., Russell, S.T., Huebner, D.M., Diaz, R. & Sanchez, J. (2010). Family acceptance in adolescence and the health of LGBT young adults. *Journal of Child and Adolescent Psychiatric Nursing, 23*(4), 205–213.

Salazar, A.M., McCowan, K.J., Cole, J.J., Skinner, M.L. *et al.* (2018). Developing relationship-building tools for foster families caring for teens who are LGBTQ2S. *Child Welfare, 96*, 75–97.

Sausa, L.A. (2005). Translating research into practice: Transgender youth recommendations for improving school systems. *Journal of Gay and Lesbian Issues in Education, 3*(1), 15–28.

Seelman, K.L. (2014). Transgender individuals' access to college housing and bathrooms: Findings from the National Transgender Discrimination Survey. *Journal of Gay & Lesbian Social Services, 26*(2), 186–206.

Seelman, K.L. (2016). Transgender adults' access to college bathrooms and housing and the relationship to suicidality. *Journal of Homosexuality, 63*(10), 1378–1399.

Selke, E., Adkins, V., Masters, E., Baipai, A. & Shumer, D. (2020). Transgender adolescents' uses of social media for social support. *Journal of Adolescent Health, 66*(3), 275–280.

Sequeira, G.M., Kidd, K., Coulter, R.W.S., Miller, E., Garofalo, R. & Ray, K.N. (2019). Affirming transgender youths' names and pronouns in the electronic medical record. *JAMA Pediatrics, 174*(5), 501–503.

Shelton, J. (2015). Transgender youth homelessness: Understanding programmatic barriers through the lens of cisgenderism. *Children and Youth Services Review, 59*, 10–18.

Shelton, J. (2016). Reframing risk for transgender and gender-expansive young people experiencing homelessness. *Journal of Gay & Lesbian Social Services, 28*(4), 277–291.

Shelton, J., Poirier, J., Wheeler, C. & Abramovich, A. (2018). Reversing erasure of youth and young adults who are LGBTQ and access homelessness services: Asking about sexual orientation, gender identity, and pronouns. *Child Welfare, 96*(2), 1–28.

Shelton, J., Wagaman, M.A., Small, L. & Abramovich, A. (2017). I'm more driven now: Resilience and resistance among transgender and gender variant youth and young adults experiencing homelessness. *International Journal of Transgenderism, 23*(2), 223–231.

Simons, L., Schrager, S.M., Clark, L.F., Belzer, M. & Olson, J. (2013). Parental support and mental health among transgender adolescents. *Journal of Adolescent Health, 53*(6), 791–793.

Singh, A.A. (2013). Transgender youth of color and resilience: Negotiating oppression and finding support. *Sex Roles: A Journal of Research, 68*(11–12), 690–702.

Steensma, T.D., McGuire, J.K., Kreukels, B.P., Beekman, A.J. & Cohen-Kettenis, P.T. (2013). Factors associated with desistence and persistence of childhood gender dysphoria: A quantitative follow up study. *Journal of the American Academy of Child & Adolescent Psychiatry, 52*, 582–590.

Stotzer, R., Silverschanz, P. & Wilson, A. (2013). Gender identity and social services: Barriers to care. *Journal of Social Service Research, 39*(1), 63–77.

Sue, D.W. (2010). *Microaggressions in Everyday Life: Race, Gender, and Sexual Orientation.* New York, NY: John Wiley & Sons.

Tannehill, B. (2019). *Everything You Ever Wanted to Know About Trans (But Were Afraid to Ask).* London: Jessica Kingsley Publishers.

Thaler, C., Bermudez, F. & Sommer, S. (2009). Legal Advocacy on Behalf of Transgender and Gender Nonconforming Youth. In G. Mallon (ed.), *Social Work Practice with Transgender and Gender Variant Youth* (pp.139–162). New York, NY: Routledge.

Turban, J.L., King, D., Carswell, J.M. & Keuroghlian, A.S. (2020). Pubertal suppression for transgender youth and risk of suicidal ideation. *Pediatrics, 145*(2), 1725–1741.

US Department of Health & Human Services, Administration on Children, Youth & Families (2011, April 6). *Information Memorandum ACYF-CB-IM-11-03, Lesbian, Gay, Bisexual, Transgender and Questioning Youth in Foster Care.*

Wahlig, J.L. (2014). Losing the child, they thought they had: Therapeutic suggestions for an ambiguous loss perspective with parents of a transgender child. *Journal of GLBT Family Studies, 11*(4), 305–326.

Wallien, M.S. & Cohen-Kettenis, P.T. (2008). Psychosexual outcome of gender-dysphoric children. *Journal of American Academy of Child & Adolescent Psychiatry, 47*(12), 1413–1423.

Wilber, S., Ryan, C. & Marksamer, J. (2006). *Best Practice Guidelines: Serving LGBT Youth in Out-of-Home Care.* Washington, DC: Child Welfare League of America.

About the Author

Gerald P. Mallon, DSW, is the Julia Lathrop Professor of Child Welfare and the Associate Dean of Scholarship and Research at the Silberman School of Social Work at Hunter College in New York City.

For more than 45 years, Dr. Mallon has been a child welfare practitioner, advocate, educator and researcher. Dr. Mallon was the first child welfare professional in the United States to research, write about and develop programs for LGBTQ youth in child welfare settings. He has also written extensively about trangender and gender-expansive youth.

Dr. Mallon's scholarship and practice has been recognized through multiple awards, including the Judge Richard Ware Award—Louisiana Children's Trust Fund; the New York State Citizens Coalition for Children Advocacy Award; the Hostetter-Habib Award, Family Equality Council; and the Child Advocate of the Year Award—North American Council on Adoptable Children. In 2014, he was also inducted as a Fellow of the American Academy of Social Work and Social Welfare. In 2020, Dr. Mallon was awarded a Champion for Children Award by the Child Welfare League of America.

He is the Senior Editor of the professional journal *Child Welfare*, and the author or editor of more than 28 books. His most recent publications are *Social Work Practice with Lesbian, Gay, Bisexual, and Transgender People* (third edition), published by Routledge, and *LGBTQ Youth Issues: A Practical Guide for Youth Workers Serving Gay, Lesbian, Bisexual, Transgender, and Questioning Youth* (third edition), published by CWLA Press.

Dr. Mallon has lectured and consulted extensively throughout the United States, and internationally in Argentina, Australia, Canada, Chile, Cuba, Hong Kong, India, Indonesia, Ireland, Israel, Mexico, the

Netherlands, Norway, Portugal, Singapore, Switzerland and the United Kingdom.

Dr. Mallon earned his doctorate in Social Welfare from the City University of New York at Hunter College, and holds an MSW from Fordham University and a BSW from Dominican College.

Correspondence may be sent via email to gmallon@hunter.cuny.edu.

Subject Index

Author Index